Creating Your Dream

Creating Your Dream

Confidently Stepping Into Your Own Brilliance

Christopher Dorris

iUniverse, Inc.
New York Lincoln Shanghai

Creating Your Dream
Confidently Stepping Into Your Own Brilliance

iUniverse books may be ordered through booksellers or by contacting:

iUniverse
2021 Pine Lake Road, Suite 100
Lincoln, NE 68512
www.iuniverse.com
1-800-Authors (1-800-288-4677)

ISBN-13: 978-0-595-31576-5 (pbk)
ISBN-13: 978-0-595-81708-5 (cloth)
ISBN-13: 978-0-595-76390-0 (ebk)
ISBN-10: 0-595-31576-3 (pbk)
ISBN-10: 0-595-81708-4 (cloth)
ISBN-10: 0-595-76390-1 (ebk)

Printed in the United States of America

For my mother,
Rosemary Dorris

Contents

Acknowledgments

Thanks to:

Andy Paschall, for the initial push.

Alison Arnold, the true founder of Head Games, for everything!

Cheryl Walsh, Walshcomm, for accountability.

Jim Myers, my Secret Weapon, for being amazing.

Chris Sandara, my brother, for your creative input, availability, uncensored feedback, and most of all, for laughter.

Introduction

This book is about creating dreams. It is simultaneously about eliminating the suffering that coincides with not pursuing your perfect life. It is written for anyone who has a Dream, or anyone who wishes to find the inspiration to create one. It is inspired by the needless suffering that most people experience for the duration of their lives. It is inspired by the miraculous transformations that occur when we discover and remove the limiting beliefs that are the source of such suffering. This book is about personal freedom—the freedom to live abundantly and without shame, reluctance or anything else short of bliss. It is about recognizing our lives as playgrounds of infinite possibilities and remembering how to play. It is about taking back power and being able to laugh at ourselves for ever having given it away. It is about taking back what is rightfully ours—joy and abundance. It's about creating and celebrating success in every form and empowering those around us to do it as well. It's about returning to our natural state—doubtlessness.

This book is about BELIEF. It's about rekindling and strengthening our belief that every one of us can live precisely how we want to live. That very belief is the birthplace of excitement and enthusiasm. You'll need them both in order to create your Dream.

This book is about remembering universal truths, embracing them and applying simple, natural skills to the creation process. It is my belief that when we are born, each of us has everything we will ever need in order to create the life of our dreams. It's all there from the start. Thus, we need not learn it. Rather, we must deprogram, or unlearn that which prevents us from acting on it. We must unlearn doubt. Each of us is born immensely powerful. Over time, however, we are all educated about our limitations. Consequently, we learn to downplay our brilliance. We learn that it is more popular and preferable to blend in and to downplay our own unique brilliance than it is to develop it with pride. We learn about impracticalities and impossibilities. We learn that what we want and the likelihood of us becoming great at anything is small. The infinite irony in that is that each of us is already brilliant and powerful. We don't need to become that. We simply need to learn how to confidently step back into our brilliance.

There is an old story—you may have heard it—about Michelangelo's statue of David. The story is a perfect metaphor for this process of "unlearning".

Michelangelo had just finished the statue David and the town was all abuzz with rumor that something miraculous had been created. Upon hearing that, one gentleman went to witness the spectacle for himself and upon viewing the statue found himself in absolute awe of its size, precision, and overall magnificence. This gentleman instantly committed himself to finding Michelangelo so that he might ask him personally how he managed to create a sculpture of such magnitude and beauty out of one of earth's hardest substances, granite. He found Michelangelo, and asked his question. He said, "Michelangelo, David is a miracle. He is absolutely breathtaking and astounding. The precision and attention to detail is incomprehensible! How in the world did you manage to create something so beautiful and so large, with so much detail out of some huge amorphous block of rock?" Michelangelo smiled humbly and replied to the gentleman, "Actually, it was quite simple. I didn't create David, you see. David already existed concealed within the stone. All I had to do was chip away at what wasn't David."

This book is about the chipping away at that which is not you— doubt, fear, limiting beliefs, guilt, discouragement, suffering.

This book is also about discipline and disciplined action. It is about the simultaneous process of strengthening your mind and taking wise action. Developing mental toughness is of no value if it is not accompanied by disciplined action. And action brought forth by an undisciplined mind will result in your returning again and again, incessantly, to the same place. It is for this reason that this book will provide you with many exercises to complete and Mental Toughness Training technologies to learn and embrace as you go forward on your path. These exercises and technologies are the "tools" that you will use to chip away. They will make up the content of your Mental Toughness workouts. They are the tools you will use to discover, eliminate and replace old limiting beliefs and habits with new expansive and abundant beliefs and habits. You will use these tools to discipline your thoughts, your emotions and your reactions. You will use them to convert adversity into fuel, to pre-program your nervous system to significantly increase the likelihood of perfect outcomes, to create pre-performance routines that guarantee perfect mind-frame for show time, to become immune to distraction and maintain laser-like focus, to stretch your personal expectations of yourself and your ability, to eliminate worry—the archenemy of all Dreams, to surround yourself with the people that make it effortless to succeed, and to revise your approach in timely and strategic ways to ensure your Master Plan has not grown obsolete.

These are the tools you will use to create your dream and confidently step into your own brilliance.

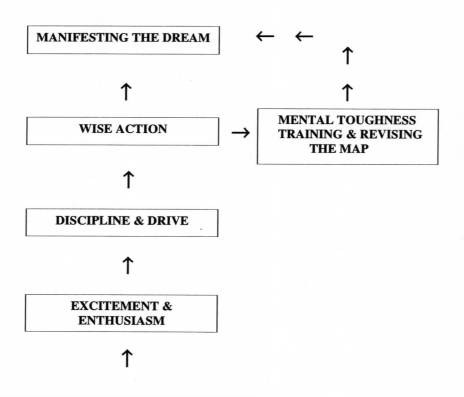

The book is organized into 3 sections, or **3 Steps to creating your Perfect Life:**

Step 1: **Know Exactly What You Want!**

Knowing what you want is the starting point. You cannot pursue your Dream if you do not know what it is.

Step 2: **Take Immediate Action & Create The Master Plan!**

Momentum is critical. In Step 2 you initiate immediate action toward the Dream and then create mindful Master Plans for continued execution.

Step 3: **Mastering Mental Toughness Technologies To Strengthen Your Approach**

It is imperative that your ongoing action be born of a disciplined mind. The third section of the book includes a list of Mental Toughness Training Technologies. These are the tools that you will master and consequently use to make your journey more efficient and more fun. These are the tools that the world's top athletic and corporate performers use to achieve consistent peak performance. The 3rd and final Step is learning and embracing these tools to continuously strengthen your approach.

How To Use This Book

It's been a year and a half since the first version of this book was published. In that time, I have heard many stories from people who have used these exercises and mental toughness tools to create powerful change in their lives. I have heard stories of people accomplishing things they would have otherwise written off as impossible, or at least impractical. Stories of people pursuing careers or new careers for which they previously considered themselves under-qualified or incapable of pursuing. Stories of people profoundly reorganizing their lives to make room for the things they most cherish—things they formerly thought unrealistic. Countless stories of people no longer waiting to start their dream businesses; teenagers and adults alike no longer waiting to pursue lifelong fantasies of professional sports careers; enormously successful attorneys becoming actors; stories of people re-establishing passion for their current professions and shining in ways they never considered possible; nationally acclaimed golf instructors creating time to get pilots licenses and learning to play guitar and sing publicly in bands; people learning to speak other languages; others creating the opportunities to fulfill their world travel fantasies; seniors getting in better physical condition than they thought possible; people no longer waiting to rekindle relationships with estranged loved ones; stories of people no longer waiting to feel expert, to feel deserved, to feel joy! They are all stories of people no longer waiting to experience or include in their lives the things they longed for and intuitively knew they could have, but didn't know how to manifest.

These are stories of the people who have taken the time to actually do this book as opposed to read it.

This is not a book that you pick up and think to yourself, "Oh, this is pretty short. The print's big. I can probably whip through this one quickly." It's not a book you read cover to cover, put down and say, "That was nice. Some good ideas in there. I should use some of that." No. This is a book that you DO. It's a compilation of exercises that you complete and mental conditioning tools that you embrace and incorporate into your daily life. Once you've completed and embraced and integrated them—over and over again—they become a personal system of achieving and maintaining clarity on what you want your life to be and taking disciplined action to create exactly that.

If you are genuinely interested in taking back your natural power and utilizing that power to create the life of your dreams, then do not simply read this book. DO THE BOOK! It is a book of action. Do not permit yourself to say, "I'll come back to that exercise and do it later." Do it now. If you do not have an hour or two right now to mindfully and thoroughly complete Exercise #1: Creating the Dream, then put this down and come back to it when you have made the time.

Once you have completed all the exercises and have finished the book, keep it with you. Keep it accessible. The process of Creating Your Dream involves quite a bit of reprogramming old thinking habits. This takes repetition. Developing psychological strength is no different than developing physical strength in that it requires repeated, ongoing trips to "the gym", so to speak. Keep the book handy and refresh yourself daily by re-reading, re-executing and reintegrating one chapter a day—until the tools have become engrained habits.

These exercises and tools—when utilized well—change lives. We evolve over time. And so do our dreams. So months down the road, do them over again—as if for the first time. When you do, you will notice yourself creating enormous, powerful change in your life. You will notice yourself creating the life of your dreams. You will witness yourself stepping further and further, confidently, into your own brilliance.

Don't just read this book. DO IT!

For those of you uncertain of your Dream, fear not. Do NOT put this book down! This is as much for you as it is for the person who has had the crystallized vision since age 2. This process is not about having it all mapped out in advance. This is about clarifying precisely what it is that you want, remembering how to even answer the question, "What do you want?" honestly and completely, and then taking immediate action to create forward progress or momentum. From that, your Dream and your path will spontaneously emerge. Do not concern yourself with choosing the "right" Dream. Instead, be committed to disciplining your mind and taking disciplined action. The rest will take care of itself!

Step 1: Know Exactly What You Want

You can only pursue what you want if you know what you want.

When I meet with folks for their very first Mental Toughness Training session, the very first question I ask them is, "What's your Dream?" I've been asking people that question for years and to date, I have yet to encounter an adult who has answered that question honestly and completely on their first attempt. Instead, they provide a response that actually comes nowhere *close* to what they actually dream of for their future. The answers are perfect answers, don't get me wrong. It's not like these people are a bunch of liars. They're just answering the wrong question. They're answering questions like, "What do you think might possibly be in store for you in the future if you get lucky and things really go your way?" Or, "What's something you think would be pretty cool?" But neither of those are the question I ask. I ask, "What's your Dream?" And it is amazing that it is so difficult for people to answer that question. Why is this? It's that we're simply out of practice. We're much better at answering a question like, "What are you afraid of?" And why is that so much simpler? Same reason. We've rehearsed answering that one. We've forgotten, as we've grown, to keep clear in our minds what it is that we want. We stink at answering the simple question, "What do you want?" How ludicrous is that? Well, we need to change that. Let's talk about why this is so important for a moment and then we'll move on to creating your very own Dream.

Your Dream is your destiny. It is the destination toward which you are traveling. And you're always traveling. As life continues, our lives evolve. We are always in motion, always evolving, always traveling—so to speak. So, where are you going? Do you know? Are you steering your ship, or are you adrift? If you are not navigating your life, it continues to evolve, but you are not exercising your choice on where to go. You have a say in where your life goes! Exercise that say. Or never ever complain about another thing; never wish—ever again—something or someone or some condition in your life to be different. You have a choice—a choice in whether or not to exercise your ability to steer your destiny—your life. If you choose not to steer, that's perfectly fine—on the one condition that you never again complain about another thing or wish for something to be different ever again. Ever. Or, you can choose to choose. You can choose to decide where your life goes and you can enjoy guiding its course.

All day long we're exercising this choice with decisions involving things like, what to wear today, what to eat and when, which pair of shoes to buy, whether or not to return a call, how fast or slow to drive, when to go to sleep and when to get up again for another day of decision making and destiny guiding. We are constantly in the process of making decisions that have to do with getting what we want. So why not exercise and apply that exact skill toward creating the future you want?

Exercise #1: Creating the Dream

The purpose of this exercise is to strengthen your ability to answer the question, "What do you want?" You can only pursue what you want if you know what you want. Permit yourself to use your most brilliant childlike imagination in doing this. By the very nature of this exercise, you must allow yourself to fantasize. Be impractical. Be unrealistic. Think big. You'll be answering the following question:

"If you were given the power to simply choose exactly and precisely what your life looked like—your Dream Life—in 2 or 3 or 5 or 10 years, what would that life be?"

No limits. As you record your fantasy, notice your trickster mind playing games with you. Notice how it says to you, "That's ridiculous", "that's clearly not possible" or "that's stupid!" Simply notice that voice and do not respond to it by adjusting or compromising your fantasy. If you want to be the CEO of a Fortune 100 company, write that. If you want to be the world's best romance novelist, write that. If you want to be a billionaire—write it. If you want to be the most compassionate human ever to have lived, write it. If you want to be 6" taller, write it. If you want to be in perfect health, free of all worry, have the power to manifest Philly Cheesesteaks with mushrooms and a Heineken at the snap of a finger…write it. If you want a deceased relative or loved one to be alive again, write it down. Remember, this is NOT an exercise in considering and recording what we think is possible. This is an exercise in removing the filters that exist in our minds that prevent us from experiencing absolute clarity on what it is that we want. Before we set about the task of going after the life of our dreams, we'd better be clear first on what that even looks like! Think Big. Think Free. What do you want?

Do this exercise NOW! Don't wait! Don't tell yourself you'll do it later. Do it now and take as much time as you need to do it well. It may take you 20 minutes; it may take 2 hours. Simply honor the process and permit yourself to set aside what you've learned about impracticality and impossibility. Use the space provided below or use a separate page to list everything you can imagine in response to the question. Keep your comments concise. You will be elaborating on them later.

"If you were given the power to simply choose exactly and precisely what your life looked like—your Dream Life—in 2 or 3 or 5 or 10 years, what would that life be?"

Consider how you want to be:
- Physically
- Professionally
- Socially
- Financially
- Romantically
- Intellectually
- Spiritually
- Emotionally

What do you want to own?

How will you be spending your time?

How will you be giving back to the world?

-

-

-

-

-

-

-

-

-

-

-

-

-

-

What you have just done is huge! Most people will go through their entire adult lives never having taken the time to do what you just did. You have just gone to the effort of asking yourself, and answering the question, "What do I really want for my life?" Do not underestimate the power of the action you have just taken. It is a simple question— one of the most important questions you can ever ask yourself—and a difficult one to answer. So difficult that you can assume that your first response falls well short of your truth. But do not be discouraged by that. It takes repeated efforts to get to your truth. Michelangelo did not take only one blow at the granite block and suddenly David appeared. It takes repeated efforts to get to your truth. That's the process. In fact, be extremely encouraged. By simply entertaining what you have just envisioned for yourself, you have already put wheels in motion that are turning and activating your unconscious. You have already begun the process of Creating Your Dream!

Do not concern yourself with the thought that some of it may appear to be absolutely impossible to attain. That's irrelevant. Throughout the remainder of this book, you will be reminded to keep your attention focused upon what it is that you *want*—not what you can't have. By doing so, you are activating all of your powers—physically and psychologically—to create your Dream. The more you contemplate your Dream, the more rapidly and efficiently it materializes. For that reason, I strongly recommend you create one or several symbolic representations or reminders of your Dream. For instance, you might create a painting or a sculpture that artistically captures your Dream, or at least an element of it. You may clip out a magazine picture that reminds you of your Dream and place it on your bathroom mirror. You may leave a copy of this exercise on your nightstand and read it every morning and night. You might laminate a copy of your Dream list and keep it in a visible place at work. You might make a collage or commission an artist to create something for you. You may do several of these things. Whatever you choose, create some method of reminding yourself of your Dream daily—so you keep it fresh and in focus.

Step 2: Create Momentum by Taking Immediate Action!

"So what lies undone
is your Kingdom come.
Chase it way down low;
It's only Love.
Don't wait until tomorrow…
Bring it on!"

—Seal

momentum: the impetus of an object in motion.

You do not need a formal plan to get started! Step #2 is all about getting moving—taking the Dream from an idea to a reality. It's about not waiting. It's about taking action—NOW! It's about creating momentum—or forward progress—so you start to create results. Some of these results will be wonderful. Those will instantly become sources of reinforcement to continue. Other results won't be so wonderful. These will serve as sources of information—information for you to utilize in the revision of your action planning later on. Information. That's all. No failure—just information. More on that later.

You must begin to create results instantly. And that's easy. Just take ⌐ Do something. Anything. Don't contemplate it forever. Just ⌐w moments you will put this book down and go do something—or a few things—toward creating your Dream. Do NOT analyze your action. Just take it. Deliberate planning will follow. And after that, the entire remainder of the book contains Mental Toughness Tools that you will learn and put to use to strengthen your execution of those deliberate plans. But don't you worry about that right now. Just act.

Pick an item from your Dream list that really excites you. Don't concern yourself with whether or not it seems difficult, far fetched, or immediately unattainable (or even entirely unattainable). Just pick one that gets you juiced.

If the most exciting item on your Dream list is to own a fishing yacht, go online right now to start pricing and shopping. Do it! If the most exciting item is to travel to all 7 continents, right now go plan a trip. Even if you don't think you'll be able to take it any time soon, go plan it. Now! If the item that gets you most jazzed is being in terrific physical shape—go join a gym or hire a personal trainer. Now! If it involves making a significant difference in the lives of children, go make a call. Volunteer. Now! Don't make excuses for waiting. Just do it. Get started.

The number one mistake that people make in pursuing Dreams is that they wait. They hesitate. For any number of reasons. Don't do it. Do not permit the undisciplined part of your brain to tell you why you can't or why you shouldn't. Take immediate action. Right now it doesn't matter whether or not you think the steps you're taking are the most rational or the straightest line approaches. As you follow Step #3 and master the Mental Toughness Technologies, you'll be taking great care of that. What's important now is that you create momentum. The value of feeling forward progress is immeasurable. Any action you take—even leaving a message on the voicemail of a travel agency regarding obtaining information on a trip you have no idea when you'll have time to go on or the money to pay for—is GOOD. It's smart. It's progress. Momentum. The information you get from that travel agent brings you closer to that trip. The phone call is what will lead to getting that information. You're closer to taking the trip you've dreamt of for so long. You've created forward progress!

Before moving on to The Master Plan (the second part of Step 2)—if you haven't already done so, go take some action. Go create some momentum!

The Master Plan

You did not need a formal plan in order to get started and create some initial momentum. You just needed to take some action. Now you *do* need a formal plan. In order to keep the momentum going, and to accelerate it, you must create your specific, planned approach to creating your Dream—The Master Plan. Here's how it works...

From your Dream list in Exercise #1, choose 3 or 4 top priorities. By priorities, I mean those items that genuinely excite you the most. What that does NOT mean are the items you think are most possible, easiest, or the ones you think you "should" be pursuing first. To keep momentum growing, you must do as Joseph Campbell advised: Follow Your Bliss!

By prioritizing the things that make you <u>feel</u> the best, you ensure emotional investment. That's motivation. If you start by pursuing the things you feel less excited about, you become more prone to burnout or total loss of momentum. Presumably, everything on your list is at least a little bit exciting to you. So this is likely not a major concern here. Simply choose the 3 or 4 items that leave you feeling the most excited.

One key to remember here: people do their best—they shine their brightest—when they're doing and pursuing what they love. This doesn't have to be difficult. In fact, it's just the contrary. By prioritizing what you feel best about, you're making it easy to create forward progress. That forward progress then increases your momentum. That increased momentum then makes it easier for you to continue to take action. So begin with what gets you jazzed.

As you go through your list to select the priorities, notice that your trickster mind may tell you things like, "No, don't pick that one, that one's way too hard," or, "skip that one for now, it's totally unrealistic." Don't listen to that voice. Your objective here is to choose the ones you *feel* most excited about—regardless of your impression of how difficult or even possible it may be. It might turn out that one or two—or even all of the items you select are items that will take quite a while to attain or completely realize. That's fine! Remember, what's important now is to create forward progress. Trust the power of forward progress! It leads to events and opportunities that you couldn't have possibly predicted. Even if it means choosing something that is absolutely *impossible* to achieve, like being able to hold your breath underwater indefinitely—fine! If that excites you, pick it. You have no idea where your action on that item will take you right away, but it will most definitely take you somewhere. And that somewhere will be just where you want to be. For example, maybe you'll end up researching free divers and their ability to hold their breath for long periods of time. Then maybe you'll end up trying free diving and loving it, or maybe you'll find yourself loving SCUBA diving as a result of all this—who knows? Just follow it. Good things inevitably come from it.

Once you've selected your top 3 or 4 priority items, write them in the spaces at the tops of the following pages and complete the exercise. The finished product: you will have a specific Master Plan for each of your initial priorities, and you will be well on your way toward creating your Dream.

Example:

Priority 1: **Start my own business**

Timeline: **2 years**

Specific Action Steps	Timelines
• interview entrepreneur friends	have 3 done by end of month
• decide company name	by Friday of next week
• decide company location	month 3, year 1
• create business plan	by January 31st
• find business plan template	tomorrow
• quit current job	month 9, year 2
• start business savings account for start-up capital	tomorrow

Of course there are more action items involved in starting a business than are listed in the example above, but this gives you an idea of what the exercise is asking from you. Be as specific as possible with your action items, and with your timelines. List as many action items as you can think of and be sure to include steps that require immediate action. Attach a timeline to every last one. It may be difficult to assign a timeline to certain items. Do your best.

Exercise #2: Master Plans

Priority 1:

Timeline:

Specific Action Steps	Timeline
•	
•	
•	
•	
•	
•	
•	
•	
•	
•	

Priority 2:

Timeline:

<u>Specific Action Steps</u>   <u>Timelines</u>

-

-

-

-

-

-

-

-

-

-

Priority 3:

Timeline:

Specific Action Steps	Timelines
•	
•	
•	
•	
•	
•	
•	
•	
•	
•	

Priority 4:

Timeline:

<u>Specific Action Steps</u>   <u>Timelines</u>

-

-

-

-

-

-

-

-

-

-

Keep your Master Plans somewhere safe, accessible and visible. Refer to them daily to make sure you are keeping your timeline commitments and to keep fresh on your next action items. When you complete an action item, replace it with another and put a timeline on that as well. Continue this process, for as long as it takes, until you realize the priority. Continuously refer to your Dream list and create Master Plans for other Dream list items, as you are inspired to do so. And you will be inspired.

Step 3: Mental Toughness Training

Now that you've created your initial momentum, and put your Master Plans in place, it's time to focus on developing Mental Toughness. The 3rd Step to creating your Dream—and the remainder of this book—is about developing absolute belief in the inevitability of your Dream! You've got the ball rolling now. You know exactly what you want. You've taken immediate action. You've created Master Plans for several items from your Dream list. The next step is to do everything in your power to keep the ball rolling, to increase its momentum and to discipline your mind so that you may use it well to accelerate the process.

What follows is a collection of tools—Mental Toughness Tools—that stellar performers from all disciplines use to manifest success. These are tools that are used regularly and literally incorporated as ways of living by the Michael Jordan's and the Jack Welch's of the world. These are tools that you too will use to develop the Mental Toughness necessary to keep your momentum going. This Mental Toughness will enable you to navigate your way efficiently through the minefields of obstacles that keep the vast majority of humans motionless—stopped in their tracks. By practicing these tools you will learn to develop unrestricted belief. You'll actually redevelop the kind of belief in yourself you had as a young child—before you were educated about your limitations. This is the kind of belief—pure knowing—that characterizes the winners of the world, like Lance

Armstrong, Champion of 6 consecutive Tours de France and cancer survivor, and Fred Smith, brainchild and chairman of FedEx.

You'll also learn how to discipline your thoughts in such a way that you convert events formerly seen as adverse into fuel. You'll learn how to discover underlying beliefs that dictate how, and if, you act. You'll learn how to reprogram those beliefs. You'll learn how to surround yourself with people who make it easier for you to succeed and live the way you want to live. You'll learn to model the attitudes and behaviors of the ones who "get it done". And you'll learn to revise your map—to recreate your Dream when the time is right, and to redirect and choreograph your Master Plans accordingly. You'll develop the attribute shared by all those who succeed in creating their perfect lives—Mental Toughness.

A List of Mental Toughness Tools

Developing Unrestricted Belief

Disciplined Thinking

Game Face

Imagery

Mental Prep Routines

Reprogramming and Reinforcing

Hoping to Knowing

Acting As If

Dialing In: Managing Distraction

Mental Stretching

Trusting Timing

The Winner's Circle

Negativity Immunity

Think!

The Secret Weapon: Your Mentor

Giving back

Great Expectations and Infinite Acceptance

Awareness and Presence

Revising the Map

Developing Unrestricted Belief

"Man, by and large, becomes what he thinks of himself."
—William James

Spring break 1990:

I was mountain biking the Slick Rock Trail in Moab, Utah. Moab is a mountain biker's Mecca, as the Slick Rock Trail is a miles long loop of surreal looking petrified sand dunes, washes, mountains, caves and canyons. It's a biking experience to be taken seriously— "for advanced riders only"—as the sign at the entrance reads. I had no place being there!

My college roommate, Chris Bingman, who lived in Utah at the time, and was very familiar with Moab and the trail, brought me there. He's one of those rare individuals who masters everything he comes in contact with—instantly. I am not. And I definitely could have been in better shape for that trip. At any rate, I was there and I was getting into it. There were some hills that were too steep to climb for my level of conditioning at the time and some too steep to descend on the bike for my level of courage—so I walked those. But the majority of them were manageable and after a while my confidence was on the rise and I became increasingly comfortable with taking some risks. I saw a steep climb that was just off the marked trail and I decided I wanted to try to conquer it. What I didn't realize was that once I had committed to it, there was no turning back.

As I rode out a narrow path to the base of this hill, I suddenly realized I had passed any point where I could change my mind. On my right was the monster hill, and now to my left was a monster chasm—a canyon that was large enough that it didn't matter exactly how deep it was—if I went that way, I'd die. For a very brief moment I recall thinking to myself, "this one's too steep for me to ride up, and it's so steep that if I lay the bike down now I'll slide off the cliff. It's too steep for me to turn around without falling and sliding into the abyss..I'm dead!" The next thing I knew—moments later—I was standing with my bike at my feet, my hands on my knees gasping for breath at the top of the monster hill wondering how the hell I got there! I made it up. I somehow summonsed the strength from an internal reservoir of power to pedal up the hill that I thought was too steep for me to summit. My companions were not nearby, so there was no one to share that experience with immediately. And I'm glad for that now. It gave me time to stand there and regain my breath and let the magnitude of what just happened sink in. Faced with falling off a cliff, and the strong possibility of death, my brain and my body coordinated to somehow find much more strength than I thought I had. That event changed my life.

From that moment on, I committed to exploring potential and the "untapped reservoir" in each and every one of us. I committed to researching and understanding what enables some of us achieve excellence while others struggle sometimes for their entire lives.

In the following chapters, I will share with you my observations thus far. I will discuss what I have found through my work with world-class athletes and CEOs, to be the key ingredients of the winners. Let's start by considering what lies at the foundation of all achievement: **Belief.**

Belief is the bottom line. It dictates everything. Your beliefs determine how your life unfolds. That's why we must begin this process of Mental Toughness Training with an exploration of your current beliefs and determine which of them are propelling you forward—toward your Dream—and which are holding you back.

It is important to remember that your natural mental state is a state of full belief. This state is characterized by a complete absence of doubt. When we are born, we are doubtless. Doubt is a construct, an idea, and it is taught to us. We start learning at a very young age how to consider the possibility of not getting what we want and then how to prioritize that consideration over the possibility of success—or getting what we want. We have literally mastered doubting ourselves by the time we enter adulthood. We have become well "educated" on our limitations!

The good news: we can unlearn doubt. We can literally re-master confidence and certainty. Our collective life experience has shaped our belief systems profoundly. It was not until my adult life studying psychology in undergraduate and graduate school that I was introduced to the possibility of reprogramming my beliefs and literally taking charge of my brain. That is the first step in creating and realizing a Dream—becoming aware of your choice or your say in what your beliefs are, and exercising that choice to dictate them. Recognizing that you even have the option of controlling your beliefs is one of the most powerful discoveries you will make in your lifetime. After all, it is your beliefs that dictate what you go for in life and how you go for it. Your beliefs also dictate what you *don't* go for—which can be even more relevant to this process of creating and realizing your Dream than what you do go for.

For example, if I believe (for whatever reason) that I don't have what it takes (whatever I believe that may be) to be wealthy, then all of my choices that could possibly affect my degree of affluence will be guided by that belief. Chances are good that I will never become wealthy.

There are countless numbers of exceptionally naturally gifted athletes on this planet that you and I will never hear of. We will never hear of them because these particular superstars don't *believe* they're superstars. And as a result, they're not. Conversely, there are many well-known athletes who have achieved exceptional levels of success but were never exceptionally naturally talented, or better yet, had tremendous obstacles to overcome. Take, for instance, Hope Lewellen. Hope lost her leg in a terrible work-related accident. Soon thereafter, Hope was playing wheelchair tennis in the 1996 Paralympics in Atlanta where she won a Silver medal in doubles! Then she went on to compete again in Australia at the 2000 Paralympics! Hope reached fourth in world rankings for wheelchair tennis players and since then has played on our National Wheelchair Basketball Team and most recently earned a spot on our National Sit Volleyball Team with whom she made her third consecutive Olympic appearance at the 2004 Paralympics! Now there's a story of someone who took enormous adversity and converted it into fuel. It's a story of a woman who focused on what she *could* do. Hope decided for herself what to believe about the loss of her leg and what that meant for her and her future. She chose her beliefs and as a result has created a wonderfully successful and rewarding life.

Dr. Herbert Benson, author of the popular books *The Relaxation Response* and *Timeless Healing: The Power and Biology of Belief*, for decades has conducted profound research studies on the power of belief and its effects on human wellness. In *Timeless Healing*, he references an experiment conducted in Japan that illustrates the power our beliefs have over our bodies.

> Just as we are warned about poison ivy, Japanese children learn to stay far from the lacquer and wax trees because of potential allergic reactions. And Japanese investigators Drs. Yujiro Ikemi and Shunji Nakagawa were fascinated by the fact that patients who merely walked under lacquer or wax trees, or by factories that process lacquer, developed severe rashes and other symptoms of dermatitis including burning, itching, and swelling.
>
> Skeptical that minute amounts of the wax or lacquer could cause such reactions, Drs. Ikemi and Nakagawa launched a study in which fifty-seven high school boys were tested for their sensitivity to the allergic substances. The boys filled out questionnaires about any past experiences with or sensitivities to the poison trees, other allergies, and their families' allergy histories. The boys were then divided into groups based on the severity of reaction they claimed to have had in the questionnaires.
>
> Boys who reported marked reactions to lacquer trees in the past were blindfolded and on one arm were brushed with leaves from a lacquer tree that they were told were leaves from a chestnut tree. They were brushed with chestnut tree leaves on the other arm but told the leaves were from the lacquer tree. Within minutes, the arm the boys believed to have been brushed with the poisonous tree began to react, growing red and developing bumps, causing itching and burning sensations, while in most cases the arm that had actual contact with the poison did not react.
>
> Skin reactions indistinguishable from actual allergic reactions were induced by *believing* contact with a poison had occurred.

Again, belief overrides reality. Belief actually determines reality. This is not true for only some of us; it is true for all of us.

Now let's begin to examine your own beliefs. The exercise that follows is the first step in heightening your awareness to the beliefs you own that dictate all of your behaviors, and consequently dictate all of your life. Take two minutes for each category below and list everything that you can think of—good or bad, expansive or limiting—that you believe to be true about that category. When you've finished, label each belief you've recorded as expansive, limiting, or neutral. A belief is expansive if thinking of it leaves you feeling excited, enthusiastic and motivated. "I'm great at what I do" and "Things are definitely going my way" are examples of expansive beliefs. A belief is limiting if it leaves you feeling restricted, doubtful, or worse yet, hopeless. For example: "I'm stuck in a dead-end career." Or, "Because I grew up in a dysfunctional, impoverished family, I'll never become a real leader or be very wealthy." A neutral belief is one that leaves you feeling neither excited nor doubtful or depressed. "I don't sing well" can be an example of a neutral belief if the fact that you can't carry a tune doesn't bother you in the least. If you have no investment in singing well, then it's a neutral belief because it doesn't excite you, nor does it upset you. It just is.

Example:

What I believe to be true about...

My Future:

- Is in my own hands   expansive
- Is uncertain   limiting
- Isn't here yet   neutral

My Past:

- Involves moments and memories I would like to forget limiting
- Is full of mistakes and traumas   limiting
- Has many great memories   expansive

Money:

- Is a source of major stress   limiting
- Is a great motivator   expansive
- Comes and goes   neutral

Exercise #3: Discovering Beliefs

What I believe to be true about...

My Future:

-
-
-
-
-

My Past:

-
-
-
-
-

Money:

-
-
-
-
-

My Intellect:

-
-
-
-

My Social Skills:

-
-
-
-
-

My Job/Career:

-
-
-
-
-

My Professional Experience/Qualifications:

-
-
-
-
-

Romance/Marriage/Family:

-
-
-
-
-

As you continue to heighten your awareness to your beliefs, you will think of others that you did not list above. Add them to your list.

This list of your beliefs is very important and you will be revisiting it later on when we discuss Reprogramming. For now, simply notice the difference in how you feel when you contemplate an expansive belief vs. a limiting belief. Soon you are going to learn how to transform your limiting beliefs and reinforce the expansive ones. But first let's take a look at your thoughts…

Disciplined Thinking

"We are what we think. All that we are arises with our thoughts. With our thoughts, we make our world."

—The Buddha

If that's true (and given the source, I'll bet it is), then the following is also true: if your thoughts are out of control, your *life* is out of control. Fairly good argument for putting some effort into taking control of your thoughts.

You choose your thoughts. You choose your thought habits. Thoughts don't just happen. No thought ever occurs to you. Nothing ever pops into your head. Nothing ever comes to mind. You create all your thoughts. All of them. Always. For most of us, however, our thought control aptitude level is currently quite low due to lack of exercise. This current thought control aptitude level is like a muscle that has atrophied as a result of a sedentary lifestyle. I call this weak mind. Weak mind is a not product of laziness. It's a result of the fact that people aren't taught to exercise their minds well. People aren't taught to choose their thoughts. Most people don't even know they have the option of choosing their thoughts. But now you do. And that knowledge comes with a great responsibility—to yourself—to your Dream.

THINK	→	FEEL	→	DO	→	RESULTS
(+)	→	(+)	→	(+)	→	(+)
(-)	→	(-)	→	(-)	→	(-)

What I think dictates how I feel. How I feel dictates how I do, how I act or how I perform. How I perform dictates the quality of my results. Consider your all-time best performances in life—sporting events, sales deals, public speaking engagements, theatrical performances, even confrontations. Think of a few specific events—stellar performances—where you absolutely nailed it. Remember them in detail. As you recall these experiences, remember how you felt during them. Recollect what your mental state was like during each performance. Chances are good that what you're recalling is one mood—and it's a damn good one! Your best performances are always characterized by you feeling great: confident, prepared, relaxed, pumped, enthusiastic, worry free, effortless, or any combination of these or any other great feeling. Now let's consider the flip side of that coin. Think of a few of your absolute worst performances of your life. Really conjure them up. As you do, remember the mood or mental state you were in during those events. Not good. It was ugly: disappointment, anger, frustration, fear, ill-preparedness, distractedness, or any combination of these or any other unpleasant feeling. Your worst performances are always characterized by feeling those sorts of things.

There's no coincidence about all this. Your great performances are great because you felt great, and you felt great because you were thinking all the right things. Your thoughts were disciplined. Your poor performances were poor because you felt poorly. You felt poorly because your thinking stunk. Your thoughts were purely undisciplined.

Notice the direction of the arrows!   THINK → FEEL → DO

One of the most costly mental mistakes that people make all the time is they wait for things to start going well before they let themselves feel great. That's backwards. That approach makes confidence contingent upon good results. Can't have that. Wastes time. It's not DO → FEEL → THINK. That would mean I must be performing well in order to ever feel great, and I must feel great in order to ever think great. Spin it around. Stop letting the outcomes dictate how you think, and start letting your thinking dictate the outcomes!

All of my actions, everything I ever do, how my life unfolds then, is dictated by how and what I choose to think! I do not control everything that happens to me, but that's OK. I don't need to. I control how I choose to interpret, or how to think about everything that happens to me. And that's all that matters.

> *"There is nothing either good or bad, until thinking makes it so."*
> —William Shakespeare

Nothing can make me sad, other than my thoughts. Nothing can make me ecstatic—with the exception of my thoughts. All mental states are products of my thinking. I control my thinking; therefore I control my mental states. This is very critical to keeping momentum flowing and accelerating. If I do not control my emotions, I am very susceptible to burnout and am likely to return to the rut. Everyday, every one of us experiences many situations in which we do not get what we want: missing a traffic light, getting a paper cut, losing a prospective deal or client, playing poorly in a game, running out of milk ½ way through pouring a bowl of cereal, poor customer service, getting 10 bills in the mail all at once, alarm clock malfunctions, plumbing situations, car trouble, long lines, dropped internet connections, lost files, screaming children on planes, an open-mouthed chewer right behind you in the movies. There are countless examples of daily occurrences of things we can, and usually do, interpret as adverse, unfortunate, unlucky, annoying, discouraging, or even disastrous. As Shakespeare said, none of these events are bad. Nor are they good. They just are—until you put the positive or negative stamp on them.

The millisecond during which you choose to interpret an event as negative (in any way) is the millisecond you choose to forfeit a tremendous amount of control over your emotions, as well as your actions. You're out of control. This is purely undisciplined. Now, how important is it for you to discipline your thoughts and choose to interpret the situation positively when you discover that you're out of iced tea mix? Not very. But it *is* very important that you choose to capitalize upon as many of these little daily situations as possible to convert disappointment into fuel. Why? For practice. So you can do it when it matters. So that when you find yourself in a do or die moment, you're well trained and can handle it. So that when your boss tells you the deadline for the report—the report upon which your promotion and raise both hinge—was just bumped from two days from now to two hours from now, you remain in control and get it done. So that when the middle reliever blows a five run lead, walks the bases loaded in the bottom of the ninth, and the coach puts you on the mound—you remain in control and get it done. And not just get it done, but get it done with poise and greatness.

THINK → FEEL → DO → RESULTS

Event: Your boss bumps up your deadline from two days to two hours. You now have two options on how you're going to interpret that.

Option A: "This stinks! This is unfair! This is bad!"

Option B: "Fine. Bring it on! I'm ready, and I always perform well under the gun. I'm gonna nail this!"

Option A is the popular choice. Most folks tend to choose to interpret this sort of event as a serious problem, as adversity. When you choose to think that way, however, remember how that affects your mental state. Think bad, feel bad, do bad. Negative thinking consistently produces negative results. In this case, that translates into a number of possible undesirable outcomes:

- Fail to complete the report. No promotion, no raise, you get fired.
- Complete a horrible report. No promotion, no raise.
- Complete a decent report. No promotion, no raise.

Is it at all possible that you could choose to interpret this event as horrible, feel horrible and still pull it off? Nope. Absolutely, positively not. If you pulled it off, you did so for one reason and one reason only. At some point you changed your thinking. You changed from angry and panicked to focused and determined. Whether you noticed it or not, you changed your thinking. That's actually Option B: the choice to convert adversity into *fuel* and utilize it as a source of inspiration and motivation.

In Sport Psychology, there's a Mental Toughness Tool called The Shooter's Mentality. It uses the game of basketball as a metaphor for choosing Option B—or converting adversity into fuel. The player who has the Shooter's Mentality believes that during performances, nothing bad ever happens. The player with the Shooter's Mentality instantly converts every event that occurs into fuel. Michael Jordan is an excellent example of an athlete who had the Shooter's Mentality. When he was playing, he would never choose to think anything that made him feel less than infinitely confident. Say Michael goes out one night and he makes his first ten jump shots in a row. What's he thinking to himself at that point? He's thinking, "Perfect. The fact that the first ten went in guarantees the next one's going in too. Give me the ball!" Not very statistically accurate, but who cares? He's not concerned with being logical or accurate with his thoughts at this moment. He's only concerned with creating thoughts that result in feeling confident—even if that means he has to stretch the truth a little—because when he feels confident, he performs his best. Now, suppose that the next game he starts off 0 for 10. What's Michael thinking now? "I'd better start passing the ball." Wrong! He's thinking, "Perfect. The fact that the first ten missed guarantees the next one's going in. Give me the ball!" While Jordan may have inherited some excellent athletic genes, mentally he doesn't have anything that you and I don't have. What he does have on most folks, though, is experience using his mental skills. That's all. Practice.

Here are a few exercises to help you get started taking control of your thoughts, and thereby staying in control of your mental states, and thus, in complete control of how you act, respond and perform in the clutch.

1. <u>Busting Thieves</u>: catching undisciplined thoughts and reactions.

Undisciplined thoughts (that result in undisciplined reactions) are like thieves that rob you of your strength and skill. Each time you generate an undisciplined thought, you lose a bit of your power and ability. In order to create your Dream, you need every bit of your strength and skill. Therefore, with each undisciplined thought, the likelihood of creating your Dream diminishes. You cannot afford to let those thoughts get away. You must catch them.

Make a habit of noticing yourself complaining—aloud or silently to yourself—throughout the course of each day. Simply notice the thoughts or statements you make like: "Damn!" "That sinks!" "I can't believe this." "This is nonsense." "I wish I had…or hadn't…" "I can't handle this." "Now I'll never be able to…" Just notice them. By noticing them, you are automatically heightening your awareness of your thinking. Only through becoming more aware of your thoughts can you get better at controlling them. By noticing your undisciplined thoughts and statements, you are "busting" the thieves and retaining your strength and skill.

<u>Some common "thieves" to catch:</u>

This stinks!
I'm not very happy about this!
That makes me so mad!
I can't stand that!
I'm so pissed off!
I hate…
That's very disappointing.
I have no idea how I'm going to…
I'm such an idiot.
I suck.
Damn! (And all your other favorite expletives.)

2. <u>The Shooter's Mentality:</u> converting adversity into fuel.

Once you heighten your awareness to your undisciplined thoughts, and you develop some mastery at "busting the thieves", the next step is to practice transforming them from undisciplined to empowering.

Remember, the athlete with the Shooter's Mentality chooses to interpret every single play that occurs during the game in such a way that it makes him feel more confident. He converts it into fuel because he knows that when he feels great, he performs great. This is much more than taking a negative and turning it into a positive. This is about taking *everything*—adversity, neutral events, and even things that you think are already good—and making them better by converting them into FUEL.

Make it a practice to use the Shooter's Mentality with all sorts of daily events, whether they are of a professional, academic, athletic, or a personal nature.

This is a tool for practicing disciplining your thinking—*all of your thinking*—so that when you are in important situations in which you need to perform, and something unexpected happens, or something "goes wrong", you remain in control of your thoughts and your actions and your Dream.

Event	Shooter's Mentality interpretation = FUEL
Flat tire	Sweet! The last time I had a flat I ended up winning the football pool at work. (Doesn't need to be true!)
Lose a prospective big contract/client	Whenever this happens, I always end up nailing down two career deals in the same month!
Forget an appointment	This gives me a great chance to take personal responsibility, and I'm going to make it better by doing something extra special for this person.
Dentist appointment to get a cavity filled	My teeth are going to be in perfect shape in a short while.

3. <u>My Biggest Pet Peeves</u> (aka, what I complain about the most.)

List your biggest pet peeves—the things that really, really bug you. In other words, identify those situations in which you are most likely to create undisciplined thoughts. Watch for them. When you find yourself amidst one, become very acutely aware of your thoughts, and then change them! Simply choose another thought. Even if this only provides very temporary relief, it is excellent practice in disciplining your mind for those times that really matter.

For example, one of my biggest pet peeves happens when I'm driving. When I'm second or third in line to make a left turn at an intersection, and the first car doesn't pull up into the intersection while waiting for an opening, the light changes, they don't go, and we all get to wait there for another light. As I sit and explain to them aloud (in a less than flattering lecture they of course cannot even hear) how inferior their driving skills are and how inefficient it is for traffic flow for them to do that, I catch myself. After I catch myself, I change my thought. And I often change it to something like, "Why am I in such a rush? Relax." And suddenly, I feel a whole lot different.

<u>Your Biggest Pet Peeves:</u>

Game Face

What actually is a Game Face? It's a term used frequently in reference to athletes and mental preparedness. But it's also used in reference to any situation or event before which or during which it is important to control your mental state. The event could be an important business meeting or presentation, a serious discussion or perhaps a confrontation between two friends or loved ones. But what *is* this Game Face to which we refer? Well, what it is not is an actual facial expression, as its name may imply. It's actually the *mood* behind the face. The expression is a byproduct of your mood—or your mental state. It's not just any mood, however. It's the mood you are in when you are performing at your absolute peak. How you feel is a product of how you think, and you control how you think. Thus, you control how you feel—you choose your moods or mental states. Thus, you have the ability to create your Game Face—or Peak Performance Mentality—at all times!

Everyone's Game Face is entirely unique to them. A Game Face is like a thumbprint. No two are alike. To know yours, simply think of some of your greatest performances in life. They can be professional, athletic, academic or personal. Your best performances will be characterized by a very similar, if not identical, mood or mental state. That mood is your Game Face. In a moment I will ask you to recall two or three of your all-time best performances. Again, they can be performances of any nature, as long as they're examples of you performing at your absolute best. Make sure the performances you choose are specific and isolated events. For example, you may recall a specific presentation or sales call, a particular sport performance, an intense conflict or confrontation, a theatrical or musical performance. Events that spanned over a period of time like the English course you aced freshman year or the month you doubled your sales quota are too broad. You may, however, choose to pick from those periods isolated events like the oral presentation you nailed in that English class, or one particular day from that record-setting month during which you made a career-high number of new sales.

Once you've selected a few stellar performances, relive each one in as much detail as possible. Literally re-experience those events in your mind's eye and pay very, very close attention to how you *felt* during those performances. Notice the moods you experienced when you were on fire. Pay attention only to how you felt when you were performing at your peak. You may have felt especially nervous before one of the events you're recalling. Ignore that. It's not relevant. Only pay attention to what you felt once you got rolling and things were going great. Take a few moments now and relive those experiences in detail.

Now that you've brought those experiences back into the fore-front, list them in the spaces below and then choose at least six power descriptors—words that really capture the mood you were in—for each of the events. Be very selective with the words you choose. List words that genuinely capture the essence of these wonderful experiences. These are some of the most impressive performances of your life, so the words you choose to describe them should be equally impressive. Don't be reluctant to use words that seem dramatic or exaggerated. These are dramatic and exaggerated experiences! <u>The words you choose must be powerful words—not ordinary words.</u> Choose them now. Take as much time as you like.

Example:

<u>Best Performances</u>	<u>Power Descriptors</u>
Basketball game senior year vs. Pennsauken	aggressive, warrior-like, confident, rested, prepared, doubtless, determined
Insurance company keynote speech	expert, impassioned, jazzed, totally present, Buddha-like, calm

<u>Best Performances</u>	<u>Power Descriptors</u>

From your collection of words, select three that you believe most accurately and powerfully reflect your peak mental state. This can be challenging, but be decisive nonetheless. Choose three words now.

Those three words are your Game Face!

PUT YOUR GAME FACE ON!

How?

1. Go through your power descriptors one by one, and as you do, *experience them*. Know what each one means specifically in reference to you and your performance. With each power descriptor, ask yourself, "What am I like when I am _____?" And don't move on to the next one until you feel it.
2. Remember a peak performance. Ask yourself, "When was a time that I had my Game Face on?"

It's as simple as that. By doing those two simple steps, you have effectively recreated your Peak Performance state of mind—your Game Face.

When?

Whenever you need to "show up" or "get it done".
- Before an important call
- Before you walk into work
- Before you take an exam
- Before a game
- Before every golf shot
- In the middle of a list of cold calls that aren't going so well
- Before and several times during a workout
- Before you ask someone out on a date!

List situations in your life when you know you'll need your Game Face. Use the categories below that apply to you.

Professional:

Athletic:

Academic:

Personal:

Note: You may not need each of the three power descriptors for every situation you listed above. For example, my three power descriptors are Warrior, Expert and Buddha. For me, the Warrior is the blood-thirsty, relentless, never-say-die competitor. The Expert is competent, has paid his dues, knows his stuff, is the best in his field. The Buddha is unaffected, infinitely peaceful, compassionate and wise. When I'm working with a client, going into a one-on-one coaching session, I put my Game Face on, but I don't need to be the Warrior for that particular event, so I de-emphasize it. Instead, I emphasize the other two—which come in quite handy. When I'm exercising, I emphasize only the first two: Warrior and Expert. When I'm playing golf, I emphasize them all. You decide in which situations to emphasize which power descriptors. But be sure to make a habit out of putting your Game Face on—always—when it's time to *get it done!*

Imagery

imagery: creating pictures in your mind's eye.

You significantly influence how your life unfolds with the pictures you create in your mind. Your mind is constantly making images, and those images translate instantly into instructions that guide your every move. Learning to control those images translates into learning how to control the instruction sets, which then translates into taking control of your Dream.

How does this work? I have no idea! And neither does anybody else. But who cares? It works. Researchers are able to tell us about the studies they conduct that illustrate the remarkable effects of imagery upon performance. They are also capable of telling us about how our nervous system is activated by the images we create in our minds and how that activation contributes to the development of neural patterns and muscle memory. But *how* it all really happens remains a mystery. And we're perfectly OK with that aren't we, because we don't need to know how it works. It just works. You turn the key in your ignition and the car starts. You flick the switch and the light comes on. How do these technologies work? Don't know. Don't really care either. You might know. But you don't have to understand it to use it and benefit from it. What really matters is that the technologies work, that you know about them and have access to them, and that using them makes it a whole lot easier to get things done.

Imagery is a technology that is entirely accessible to every conscious being and is as powerful as any other technology available to us, perhaps significantly more so.

Your brain does not know the difference between real and imagined experience.

Your brain records and stores real events and imagined events in the exact same way. If I imagine, in detail, delivering a speech, my brain records that event as if it actually happened. Therefore, it exists in my mind as experience. It may as well have happened, then, because the stored memory of the imagined event will affect me the same way as would a stored memory of a real event.

There's a true story of a man that was a P.O.W. in Viet Nam who spent hours every day while imprisoned imagining himself playing golf with his buddies at his home course. He was using fantasy as a way to escape mentally from the horrors of being a prisoner. He imagined round after round after round of hitting great shots and playing stellar golf. He survived the experience, and when he was released he had lost 80 pounds. Naturally one of the first things he wanted to do upon regaining his freedom was go play a real round of golf. To the astonishment of his fellow officers, he played a phenomenal round. Why? As a result of all the imaginary great golf he played in his mind in the prisoner camp, he had literally trained his muscles and programmed his body to hit great golf shots. Neither his brain nor his body "knew" that all those great golf shots he imagined never actually happened.

Imagery programs your brain, and your body, to perform. By imagining greatness, you are literally increasing the likelihood of experiencing it. By creating clear images of what you want to have happen, you are instructing your brain to do everything in its power to make that image a reality.

The two keys here are:

1. Clarity

2. Perfection

The images must be clear in order for the instructions to be clear. And your brain does not discriminate between images of perfection and images of doom. Whatever you are imagining—from extreme success and joy, to extreme struggle and suffering—instantaneously begins to manifest itself. It is for this reason that you must be very disciplined with the images you create!

There are infinite applications for imagery. You can use it for creating affluence, health, confidence, athleticism. And you can utilize imagery to expedite creating what you want in both the distant future as well as in the immediate future. Here are three imagery exercises I highly recommend.

1. The Pendulum

This is an imagery training drill. It serves to strengthen your ability to image clearly. Additionally, it is an excellent exercise for intensifying focus. Get a 6" long piece of string, and tie a one ounce fishing weight to one end of it. (If a fishing weight isn't handy, improvise by using something that weighs about the same as a small battery and affix it somehow to the end of a string.) Hold the string by the index finger and thumb of your dominant hand. Rest your elbow on a table, bend your wrist so the back of your hand is parallel to the table top and if you need to, choke up on the string so the weight dangles just above the table top. Now you're ready to begin. First, create an image of the weight swinging side-to-side, left to right. Literally permit yourself to experience that happening in your mind's eye. Give yourself a good minute or two to do that. Next, change the image in your mind to see the weight swinging forward and backwards—toward you and away from you. Literally permit yourself to experience that happening in your mind's eye. Then, create an image of the weight swinging around in a circle. And finally, imagine it changing directions and rotating in a circle going the opposite direction.

Impressive, huh? The weight moved in exactly the directions you imagined. (If your weight did not move, you have a serious cognitive disorder and require immediate psychiatric attention—just kidding. If it didn't move, simply practice this some more. If there was no movement, it could only be for one reason: the images in your mind were not clear enough long enough. Practice and it will come.) The images you created of the weight moving translated instantly into instructions (from your brain to your hand in this particular case) to make it so.

Practice this exercise from time to time and concentrate on getting the weight to move farther and to respond more quickly.

2. <u>Recreating the Dream</u>

This exercise involves experiencing the future exactly as you want it to be, long before it happens. The purpose of doing this is to significantly increase the likelihood of manifesting your Dream.

In Step 1, you answered the question, "What do you want?" Your answer is your Dream. Live that Dream in detail everyday clearly in your mind's eye. Experience it vividly. Experience yourself in two years, five years, ten years, and imagine *perfection*—in every conceivable way. Imagine being exactly the kind of person you want to be, with all the qualities and characteristics you desire. Imagine your own version of perfection in all forms: physically, financially, romantically, professionally, spiritually, materially, intellectually, socially and emotionally.

Do this daily. Do not let a day go by without spending even a minute or two experiencing your perfect future. Recreate the Dream daily, and in so doing, help it unfold.

3. Pre-Performance Imagery

This involves using imagery to help you perform flawlessly—for something you are about to do in the immediate future. This is what you see Olympic downhill skiers doing on TV just prior to their runs. When you see them at the top of the hill, minutes before their turn to go, with their eyes closed and often swaying side to side in the crouch, they are actually skiing the course perfectly in their minds. They are programming their muscles for perfect performance. By imagining flawless execution immediately prior to performing, they are significantly strengthening their chances of actual flawless execution.

The following is a list of possible situations that you would want to experience—clearly and perfectly—in your mind's eye prior to execution:

- An important phone call
- A sales presentation
- An important meeting
- A round of golf
- Every golf shot
- A tennis match
- Every serve
- A confrontation
- An interview
- A theatrical performance
- A set in the weight room
- Requesting a raise/promotion
- Hiring someone
- Firing someone
- A speech
- An audition
- Asking someone out on a date
- Proposing marriage

Think of situations in your life for which you will use Pre-Performance Imagery and list them here. Even a couple short minutes of imagery can produce profound results. The more, the better, but you don't have to spend hours a day on it.

Mental Prep Routines

What do you do to ensure that you're more mentally tough with each passing day? What do you do to make sure you're perfectly mentally prepared before important performances? If you don't have a specific response for both of these questions, (and most folks don't) then this Mental Toughness Tool will be especially valuable for you. Even if you do already have daily Mental Toughness exercises and pre-performance Mental Prep Routines in place, now is as good a time as any to re-evaluate them and tune them up.

Mental Prep Routines are the psychological equivalents of physical conditioning routines and pre-game warm-ups in sports. They serve the function of conditioning your mind and creating readiness. A quick examination of today's elite corporate and athletic performers shows us that technical and physical expertise alone are not enough to achieve greatness. Mental Toughness is more important to success now than ever, and it's only becoming more so. Consider Tiger Woods, for example. There is little debate around the suggestion that Tiger is significantly more physically talented than the rest of the world's top players. There is even less debate, however, around the suggestion that he is significantly more mentally tough. This is true for all sports, and all disciplines in life. At the elite level of anything, what distinguishes the greats from the rest is not technical or physical talent or skill. The variances of those variables are negligible in comparison to the differences in degrees of Mental Toughness. This is true with respect to corporate "players" as well. Jack Welch, or "Neutron Jack" as some of his employees referred to him, one of history's greatest corporate leaders, became GE's youngest ever Chairman and CEO at 44. In his twenty years at the helm, he inflated the company's market value from $12 billion to $280 billion. He is known for his excellence in many disciplines including communication, persistence, embracing change, aggressive execution of deliberate plans, and genuine contact with employees. This is a man who understands and personifies Mental Toughness.

As performance standards continue to rise, competition becomes tougher, which means so must you—mentally. Get excited about that. Mental conditioning enhances every element of your life, not just success in the workplace or on the playing field. Possessing Mental Toughness makes everything easier. Everything.

The trick is to make your mental conditioning drills habitual—or routine. When something becomes routine, it's automatic. It becomes increasingly effortless. Effortless is good. Don't confuse effortlessness with laziness. Effortlessness is a product of diligence and mastery. When one thing becomes effortless, it frees you up to take on something more challenging.

Developing routines is as natural as breathing. You have hundreds of routines in place already in your life. Consider your morning routine, which is made up of several sub-routines. You get up and go through a series of rituals, steps you go through in just about exactly the same order, taking just about exactly the same amount of time each time. Each of these rituals is made up of steps that involve preparing you for your day—increasing the likelihood of you getting what you want out of it. And every single last one of those little steps at some point in your life required conscious effort, or may have even seemed like an inconvenience, or at the very least took some time to incorporate as habit. Kids don't shower. Not without being told to do so over and over and over. At some point us men had to start shaving, and not long after that had to start shaving daily. One more little thing to do. Just think of all the little things you do every morning to get yourself ready. When you stop to think about it, that's a lot of work. What's nice about it, however, is that you <u>don't</u> have to think about it. You just do it. You just get it done. It's automatic. It's routine.

What makes something routine? Repetition. Your Mental Prep Routines will at first, like anything else, take effort. But soon (some researchers say 24 consecutive days of repeating a behavior makes a habit—I think it can be done in less) you'll be executing your daily Mental Toughness conditioning drills effortlessly.

There are two types of Mental Prep Routines:

1. The Daily Mental Toughness Training Routine (DMTTR)
2. Pre-Performance Routines

1. The Daily Mental Toughness Training Routine:

This is the answer to the question, "what do you do to ensure that you're more Mentally Tough with each passing day?" It's your daily mental workout. Give yourself about five to ten minutes of uninterrupted private time for this.

Execute the following 5 steps in order:

1. Recreate The Dream: Experience your Dream in detail.
2. Recommit to Doing What It Takes: Creating your Dream takes commitment and sacrifice. Recommit yourself daily to making those sacrifices. Consider what sacrifices you may encounter today or tomorrow and commit fully to making them.
3. Game Face: Practice putting your Game Face on.
4. Imagery: Imagine the events of your upcoming day and experience yourself being and executing perfectly.
5. The Shooter's Mentality: Fill your mind with confidence building thoughts about your upcoming day, week, project, event, family matters, and your life in general.

2. Pre-Performance Routines:

The Pre-Performance Routine is your answer to the question, "what do you do to make sure you are perfectly mentally prepared before important performances?" Pre-Performance Routines are mental warm-ups. These are the routines you execute immediately prior to performing to ensure you go into the event in the perfect mindset.

The Pre-Performance Routine consists of the three essentials:

1. Game Face
2. Imagery
3. The Shooter's Mentality

1. Game Face: Put it on!
2. Imagery: Experience yourself executing flawlessly and being exactly as you desire.
3. The Shooter's Mentality: Flood your mind with confidence building thoughts about why this will be the best performance of your life!

Reprogramming (the Limiting Beliefs) & Reinforcing (the Expansive ones)

Being able to do anything with your beliefs first requires that you are aware of them. Beliefs are elusive. Old ones are persistent. That's OK if the beliefs are empowering ones, but if they're limiting, then the trick is to manipulate or reprogram them into empowering beliefs that work in your favor.

You may recall from our discussion in the beginning of Step 3, that your beliefs shape your world. Operating systems are to personal computers as belief systems are to humans. Your belief system dictates how you run. Fortunately, unlike present day computers, you can deliberately reprogram your OS.

In the chapter Developing Unrestricted Belief, you completed an exercise on identifying some of your beliefs about your future, your past, money, etc. You will be using your responses from that exercise in this section. From that list, you will be choosing beliefs to either reprogram or reinforce. Limiting beliefs (those that retard the progress of realizing your Dream) will be reprogrammed; expansive beliefs (those that accelerate your progress) will be reinforced.

Becoming aware of the beliefs that guide your behaviors takes practice. It requires consistent attentiveness. Your list is a great start, but it's just that. It's a start. There are many more very powerful beliefs operating in your mind that have yet to make it onto that list. As you continue to practice this skill over time, you will naturally become aware of some of these powerful and elusive beliefs. When that occurs, you will have the option of either reprogramming them or reinforcing them. The beliefs you have already identified on your list, however, are more than enough to get started on the process of reprogramming and reinforcing.

Reprogramming Limiting Beliefs

From your list, select from the beliefs you labeled as Limiting, the 3 that you feel present the greatest amount of resistance. That is, select the 3 that, if turned around, would make the greatest impact on your ability to create your Dream. You know it's a Limiting Belief if when you think about it, you feel restricted or constrained—you feel a loss of freedom.

Limiting Belief   **Reprogrammed into Expansive**

The reprogramming process is theoretically simple, but again, requires you to be persistent and alert. Limiting beliefs aren't fond of rejection and they are often a little slow to pick up on the fact that they're unwanted. It is possible that it will take several attempts to reprogram the older, more stubborn beliefs, and that's OK. That's how it works. Don't get discouraged if you notice a limiting belief that you thought you successfully reprogrammed, return in its original form. Just be firm with it, as you would an uninvited and disrespectful solicitor that repeatedly disregards your boundary setting. You do not need to react emotionally—just be firm.

An example: Let's say that I believe that money is the root of all evil. This is an extremely limiting belief. If I believe that money begets all evil, then I will consciously and unconsciously behave in ways that ensure I have little or no money. When I think about money, which is quite often, considering it is something I must use everyday in order to exist in this culture, I feel anxious. It may at times be mild, almost imperceptible anxiety, but it's there and it's costing me. It is decelerating the process of creating my Dream. Even if only a little bit, that's not OK with me. In fact, it's purely undisciplined. It must be reprogrammed.

Limiting Belief → **Reprogrammed into** → **New Expansive Belief**

Money is the root of all evil. → → **Money is good. Money gives me freedom. Money allows me to help others.**

To reprogram a limiting belief, consider it's opposite. In the example above, that's easy. The opposite of evil is good. Money makes it easier for me to be benevolent. That's an Expansive Belief, as it is accompanied by a sensation of freedom and inspiration. It compels me in a skillful way. To reprogram, I must repeat the new Expansive Belief over and over and over to myself. I must write it down and put it somewhere visible, on my dashboard for instance, or in my daytimer or PDA, or on my screensaver to remind me. Additionally, if I notice myself thinking, "Money is bad" again, I must catch myself, reprogram it in my mind again in that very moment, and repeat the new Expansive Belief as a mantra. I must repeat this process until the old limiting belief is gone for good.

Now, to complicate things. There is such a thing as an underlying belief. An underlying belief is the belief that lies beneath what you think is the relevant belief, and it's the underlying belief that's controlling you. Consider the following:

"My past involves memories I would like to forget."

This appears to be a limiting belief. But it's not really a belief. It's a wish that is born out of an underlying belief. Why would you want to forget those memories or events? You must believe that those events were bad and still affect you. That's the underlying belief. "My past involves events that were bad and they still affect me in a bad way" is the underlying belief that's fooling you into believing you'd be better off forgetting them. What if you could reprogram that into something like, "I believe every event from my past has been purposeful and has helped me become the person I'm proud to be today"? Then you'd have yourself an expansive belief. With this particular example, you may discover a series of limiting beliefs about all the specific events from your past that you believe to be bad. You can reprogram them all.

Now, using the 3 limiting beliefs you chose from your list, reduce them to their underlying beliefs, if necessary, and reprogram them into expansive beliefs.

Example 1

Limiting Belief: My future involves enormous financial stress.

Underlying Belief: none.

New Expansive Belief: **My future involves enormous financial freedom and affluence.**

Example 2

Limiting Belief: I believe my past is characterized by poverty.

Note: You could actually perceive this belief as limiting or expansive depending on how you choose to think about it. For this exercise, let's say the person possessing this belief has identified it as a limiting belief.

Underlying Belief: **Having been poor in my youth holds me back now and may continue to do so in the future.**

New Expansive Belief: **My impoverished youth provides me with invaluable motivation to create my Dream.**

Your turn…

Limiting Belief:

Underlying Belief:

New Expansive Belief:

Limiting Belief:

Underlying Belief:

New Expansive Belief:

Limiting Belief:

Underlying Belief:

New Expansive Belief:

5 Steps to Reprogramming Limiting Beliefs:

1. Identify any underlying belief, if one exists.

2. Reprogram into its opposite.

3. Make the new Expansive Belief a mantra. Repeat it over and over until it takes root. You may choose to include the mantra as a step in your Daily Mental Toughness Training Routine.

4. Create visible reminders of the new Expansive Belief.

5. Stay alert and aware: notice when and if the old limiting belief revisits. Notice when you feel restricted or anxious.

Reinforcing Expansive Beliefs

Reinforcing expansive beliefs involves 5 steps as well:

1. **Make it more powerful by strengthening the language.**
2. **Disregard whether or not the new expansive belief is entirely true.**
3. **Make it a mantra.**
4. **Create visible reminders.**
5. **Stay alert and aware of skepticism: permit the new reinforced belief to become true as a natural consequence of adopting it.**

1. Make it more powerful by strengthening the language.

In this step, you will utilize the power of language to transform an expansive belief into a tremendously expansive belief!

My future is exciting. → becomes → **My future is full of infinite possibilities and I am in complete control of it.**

My past is full of lessons. → becomes → **My past is full of lessons that make it effortless for me to create my Dream.**

| I learn quickly. | → becomes → | Because I learn quickly, my professional success is guaranteed. |

| I have good social skills. | → becomes → | My exceptional social skills ensure a perfect social life for the rest of my life. |

In the examples above, notice the difference in language and effect. Why settle for good when you can have great?

2. Disregard whether or not the new Expansive Belief is entirely true.

You might be thinking to yourself that the reinforced beliefs above are exaggerated, impractical, or even untrue. Don't worry about it! They are so by design. They need to be stretches. As a result of adopting them as beliefs, in time, they become truths.

3. Make it a mantra.

Repeat it over and over and over and over…

4. Create visible reminders.

Don't rely on memory when it comes to reprogramming and reinforcing beliefs. Write your new belief down and place it in obviously visible locations so you can't help but notice it several times throughout the day.

5. Stay alert and aware of skepticism; permit the new reinforced belief to become true as a natural consequence of adopting it.

One lesson many of us have learned, that doesn't always serve us, is that we always need to be honest with ourselves. Not always. Fairytales are not true, yet they serve a tremendous value in developing creativity, inspiration and joy. Think of these reinforced Expansive Beliefs as fairytales that, with a little nurturing, become reality.

Select a few Expansive Beliefs from your list that you would like to reinforce. List them below, and go to town.

Expansive Belief:

New Extremely Expansive Belief:

Expansive Belief:

New Extremely Expansive Belief:

Expansive Belief:

New Extremely Expansive Belief:

Hoping To Knowing

There's nothing like certainty. It's so comforting. Admittedly, it's not always as exciting as chance, but personally, I'm adequately satiated with chance in other areas of my life that I don't need it, or want it, interfering with creating my Dream. I like a good gamble as much as the next guy, but not with my Dream.

Mental Toughness is about doing everything in your power to maximize the likelihood of getting what you want. It's about reducing risk by taking control. This next Mental Toughness Tool involves increasing your odds by raising your level of certainty. The more certain you are, the less doubt you have. The less doubt you have, the better your chances.

"I'm hoping to start my own business someday."

"I'm going to run to the store to pick up some batteries."

Notice the difference between these two futuristic statements. There's a huge distinction in their degrees of certainty—or knowing. The first statement is an expression of desire. The second is a statement of fact. The first is hoping, the second is knowing. If an odds maker was going to put numbers on these two events, going to the store to get batteries would, hands down, be the safer bet. However, Mental Toughness—the mentality you want to have in creating your Dream—doesn't acknowledge odds in a conventional way. Ultimate performers determine their own odds. Remember the Shooter's Mentality from the Disciplined Thinking chapter. People with the Shooter's Mentality create their own reality (which includes their own odds) when performing. They only choose to generate thoughts that significantly increase the likelihood of success—thoughts that result in extreme levels of confidence. The discipline of transforming hoping into knowing relies upon this same willingness to dictate your own odds. It's the willingness to simply decide for yourself, despite anything you know to the contrary, that you are guaranteed to get what you want. It's not just possible. It's not just probable. It's definite!

The ways we act when we are doubtless are the most disciplined, productive, and successful behaviors we ever exhibit. When we take doubtless action, we create results. Is it possible that even though I state with absolute certainty and knowing that I am going to the store to get batteries, I won't actually succeed in doing so? Yes it is. Something unusual could happen that would prevent me from getting it done. In fact, many things could happen. I could get kidnapped. I could have an accident. I could experience rapid onset disorientation or dementia and forget who I am and where I am going. I could get abducted by aliens. It's all possible. Not likely, but possible. Despite all the possible reasons why I wouldn't succeed at getting to the store, I don't consider the possibility of not accomplishing my goal. I don't even remotely consider the possibility of <u>not</u>. And that's brilliant. That's discipline. That's Mental Toughness. *That* is how you want to think about creating your Dream! There are millions of possible reasons why you wouldn't accomplish your Dream. But you're not interested in any of them at all.

Knowing is a state of such certainty that not only do you not consider reasons why you wouldn't succeed, nor do you consider reasons why you would. You're so certain, you don't need to. It's like turning on the light. How often do you consider whether or not the light will come on? Never. Even though you have had multiple experiences in the past where the light blew and you didn't get the light you wanted, you still don't consider that the next time you go to flick the switch. You just know. And in that knowing, you act without hesitation. No reluctance. Pure belief. Purely disciplined action. It's perfect.

So how do you get from hoping to knowing?

1. You change your internal dialog.

2. You change your external dialog.

First, get into the habit of using knowing language in your self-talk.

Hoping Language	Knowing Language
I'd like to be more generous.	I am more generous now, and I'm becoming even more so.
I hope to get into the program at NYU.	I am going to attend the NYU program.
If I'm lucky, I'll get the promotion.	I'm going to be promoted.
I wish I owned a big house.	I'm going to buy my dream home.
I hope we get funding.	The funding is definitely coming.
I'd love to be a millionaire.	I'm becoming a millionaire.

Next, change your external dialog. Take some risks! If you want to become a concert pianist, and you're afraid to say that out loud, get comfortable putting yourself out on the limb. Commit. Get knowing. If you're concerned about sounding cocky or arrogant, stop. Saying, "I'm going to become the world's greatest concert pianist" isn't cocky coming from a kid. Why should you not be afforded the same privilege of dreaming big with certainty? Plus, it's no more cocky or arrogant a statement than, "Tonight, I'm going to make a lasagna, build a fire, and watch a movie." Both are statements made with certainty. If the listener chooses to hear one as arrogant, that's their deal. If your listener projects doubt onto you by labeling your disciplined thought and knowing statement as arrogant or inappropriate in any way, let them. Just don't buy into it. Smile and give them a copy of this book! That's cocky.

As you demonstrate knowing, watch for transformations in both your behaviors, and, of course, your results. When you think and speak differently, you naturally behave differently. When you behave differently, naturally your results change as well!

Acting As If

All great performers, all great achievers are also great actors. Acting is an expression of fantasy. And it's fun. Not only is it fun, it's an invaluable Mental Toughness Tool for creating your Dream.

Imagine yourself, some time in the not too distant future. Imagine that you've fulfilled your Dream completely. You're living it! Imagine that in detail. Experience it. Experience the you of the future. Perfect, in every imaginable way. Take a couple minutes to create this fantasy now.

Now imagine that you've been casted to play a major role in a blockbuster movie in the making. The character you've been chosen to play is the one you just imagined. You, of the future. So now you've got two things to do to pull this off with an Oscar winning performance:

1. Get to know the character intimately
2. Immerse yourself in the role

Character Study

Getting to know the character involves an intense examination of every nuance of his behavior, his spoken language, and his body language. Do the above imagery exercise over and over again so you acquire a <u>crystal clear</u> familiarity with the way your character thinks, speaks, dresses, walks, eats, laughs. Know how your character behaves in formal settings, in casual environments, how he spends free time, and with whom. Know how he operates professionally, socially, emotionally, spiritually, financially, athletically, intellectually. Know every move he makes. Know his body language: how he smiles, sits, postures, makes eye contact, listens.

To know this, just keep imagining yourself in the future living your Dream, and imagine many different scenarios. Play them out in your mind. Emphasize detail. Imagine yourself in every different setting that your Dream involves: professional settings, with family, socially, alone time. Make sure you place special emphasis on knowing how your character operates mentally—how he thinks. You can't imagine every possible scenario in which your character could ever find himself, but if you know how he thinks, then you can predict his behaviors in any given situation.

Immersion

Once you feel like you've come to know and understand your character intimately, the next step is to immerse yourself in the role. Become the character. Imitate him to the nth degree. Mimic his every expression, step, thought. Do it all the time. Be him at work. Be him at home. Be him when driving your car. Become him.

You are acting as if you already were this person. Naturally, the result is you become him. Your behaviors, your thinking, your expression of yourself will be that of the infinitely confident, knowing, disciplined, successful, joyful you. You're stepping into your Dream!

Answer the following two questions. Use the bullet points to record 3–5 concise responses.

How does my ideal self act differently professionally?
How does my ideal self act differently personally?

Here's an example:

How does my ideal self act differently professionally?

- he's more playful
- he's more decisive
- he acts more like an expert, he takes more risks
- he speaks more confidently

How does my ideal self act differently personally?

- he doesn't act defensive when confronted or challenged
- he doesn't worry, he just gets things done and stays in control of his emotions
- he laughs more, and tells more jokes
- he's more nurturing with his children
- he's never in a hurry; he doesn't need to be

Record your responses below.

How does my ideal self act differently professionally?

-
-
-
-
-

How does my ideal self act differently personally?

-
-
-
-
-

Now it's time to make a commitment to action. Chose two—only two (for now)—of the items you listed above, one professional and one personal, and, starting this very moment, commit to acting that way more often. What you are committing to, is to act. You are making a firm commitment to begin acting in two specific ways that will result in you more closely resembling the ideal you of the future. You are acting as if you already are that perfect you of the future.

Example:

I commit to:

- take more risks professionally
- act more worry free

Your turn:

I commit to:
-
-

Dialing In: Managing Distraction

Creating your Dream requires that you complete tasks—that you consistently execute. One of the greatest threats to consistency and disciplined execution is distraction. Our minds have such wonderful senses of humor. They're goodhearted tricksters, and they amuse themselves by wandering and roaming about. Goodhearted or not, their adventurous nature can be a real problem for us when we want to get things done and need to stay focused. Becoming great managers of distraction takes awareness and discipline. You must first be aware of the sources of distraction and that you are permitting your mind to be affected and veer off course. You then must demonstrate the discipline to act on that, decisively, to manage the distraction. Before anything else, however, you must remember at all times that you have the absolute power to control your mind, and therefore your attention. You must *believe* that it is even possible for you to do so. If you forget this, or choose to disbelieve it, you will remain a victim to distraction and your trickster mind indefinitely.

For some folks, managing distraction is more challenging than it is for others. Some people are more distractible than others. That's really no different than some folks having a naturally higher metabolism than others. It certainly should not be viewed as a weakness or a mental deficiency. It's simply different and requires a different quality of management. Some folks are more vulnerable to distraction, some are more vulnerable to bee stings, while others are more vulnerable to rapid fluctuations in blood sugar levels. These can be viewed as problems or weaknesses, or they can simply be perceived as facts. I recommend the latter.

I spent several years counseling families with children who were diagnosed with Attention Deficit Disorder (ADD). It is popular opinion nowadays, in the field of counseling psychology, that ADD is the most over-diagnosed "disorder" listed in the Diagnostic Statistical Manual. I place the term "disorder" in quotes because the term must be used with extreme caution. It was my distinct observation that people who were diagnosed with ADD were very often influenced by unqualified professionals to believe that having ADD meant that they cannot control their attention. A diagnosis of ADD does *not* mean you can't control your attention! It means it may take more disciplined and structured effort to do so. There's a big difference. The difference is in the level of belief or perceived control that the person has over their ability to concentrate. And as we discussed earlier, what you believe dictates how you take action—or whether you take action.

Regardless of whether you have been diagnosed with ADD or not, it is imperative that you believe you have the ability to control your focus. The amount of effort that you must exert to achieve and maintain such control may simply be different than that of those around you.

3 Steps to Managing Distraction

1. **Awareness**

2. **Prevention**

3. **Management**

1. Awareness

The first step is to become acutely aware of the sources of distraction to which you are most vulnerable. These sources are both internal as well as external. Internal distractions have to do with your own thoughts. External distractions are the events or stimuli that occur around you. When you are aware of your most popular distraction sources, you are significantly more capable of preventing and managing them.

Internal Distractions

External Distractions

Thoughts of:

Tasks
- what else needs to get done
- what else I could be doing

Mass Media/Communications
- TV
- radio
- print media
- internet
- phone

Fantasy

People

- "I wonder what so and so is up to."
- "What if I won the lottery?"
- "What if people had three legs?"
- Unrelated/Irrelevant creative ideas

- coworkers
- family
- friends
- teammates

Events

- entertainment
- breaks

Use the space below to list the distractions to which you are most vulnerable, both internally and externally. Take a few minutes to really think about this and record your thoughts below.

Internal   **External**

•   •

•   •

•   •

•   •

•   •

2. Prevention

Now that you've become aware of your most prevalent distractions, you can devise ways to eliminate, or at least reduce, their ability to interfere with your productivity.

Preventative measures include:

      1. Not setting yourself up

      2. Beating it to the punch

      3. Strategic scheduling

1. <u>Not setting yourself up:</u>

This is the common sense approach to reducing the likelihood of distraction. It involves doing things like turning off the phone or even going to the library instead of completing the project at the office or at home. Simply ask yourself, "Under what circumstances are the distractions above least likely to occur?" Then choose to perform under those circumstances when at all possible. For example, in executing the task of writing this book, I had to change the circumstances a few times in order to prevent tremendous amounts of distraction. When writing, I do so at home as opposed to my office to prevent distractions like phone calls, colleagues, deliveries, solicitors, and the temptation to do other projects. I turn off my telephone. I also deliberately choose music to listen to that inspires me and helps me concentrate while drowning out all other external noise.

2. <u>Beating it to the punch:</u>

Beating the distraction to the punch involves satiating distracting temptation or desire before you begin your task. Suppose you have an email checking addiction. That's fine. There are worse addictions. Check your email, and write several emails—just because—before you begin to execute your task. Suppose you have a habit of checking in or chatting with your colleague down the hall. Do so before you begin, and let them know you'll be unavailable for the next hour or so. Suppose you like to distract yourself with coffee or snack breaks. Get yourself an extra large cup and stuff your face before you set about your work. Anticipate the distraction in advance, and do what it takes to satiate the desire beforehand. If that means spending a half hour returning phone calls before you engage, so be it. Remain one step ahead of your distractions.

3. Strategic Scheduling

Always schedule your tasks, and schedule them at times when you are likely to face the fewest distractions. If I didn't schedule one day each week to write this book, I would never have finished it. I tried without scheduling time for three years! Once I scheduled the task, I finished it in a matter of a few short months.

For many folks, it's a great idea to literally schedule time for such things as reading, thinking, and even time with loved ones. If you're one of them, keep those appointments firm! There will always be multiple temptations to reschedule. Barring family emergencies, don't do it. Jack Welch, former GE CEO, commented that the most important task he ever executed was effectively managing his schedule. If you're thinking to yourself, "I shouldn't need to schedule time for things like going to dinner with my spouse or attending my kid's baseball game," challenge that thought. Who cares what you "should" or "shouldn't" need to do? If it helps you prevent distraction and consequently perform more effectively, do it.

You can profoundly reduce the likelihood of distraction by making a concerted effort to deliberately and strategically schedule your tasks.

3. Management

The third step in managing distraction is managing distraction. Is that helpful? Well, to elaborate, it is impossible to prevent all distraction, and therefore the best we can do is learn to manage well that which we could not prevent. Distractions are not bad. Not only are they not bad, often they're wonderful and valuable. Fantasy, for example, can provide us with creative ideas, inspiration and enthusiasm. I can't tell you how many times I've permitted my mind to drift off, while writing this book, into fantasies of exploring Africa, for instance, or ideas of future writings. These are valuable ideas. The key is to manage these thoughts in such a way that you can benefit from them, and at the same time compartmentalize them such that they don't compromise your productivity in the moment. Record them, and redirect your attention back to the task at hand.

Ironically, distractions can even be timely. For example, you could be working on a report when you drift off into a daydream of being the quarterback for the Philadelphia Eagles in the Super Bowl, which then transitions into a fantasy of being an eagle soaring high over the earth, which then transitions into being an astronaut, which then transitions into a fantasy of being one of the first families to colonize the moon—when suddenly you hear a loud thunderclap that breaks your train of thought. You were long gone. You could've gone on for another 20 minutes with that distracting fantasy if it hadn't been for the thunder to snap you out of it. The external distraction—the thunder—interrupted your internal distraction. It was timely. So distractions are not inherently bad things, and aren't always even undesirable, but they do need to be managed.

There are three keys to successful distraction management:

1. Internal management

2. External management

3. Picking specific targets and rewarding yourself

1. Internal Management

This is thought control. Your thoughts are like a flock of sheep. They wander because it's in their nature. You are the shepherd. Your job is to keep watch over your flock, not as much to protect them from predators as to simply keep them concentrated together. As a shepherd, when one of the sheep starts to wander off, you want to be alert enough to notice it as soon as possible and bring it back. It's the same concept with your thoughts. You want to notice, as soon as possible, when a thought begins to drift, and bring it back. Here is an exercise to practice such thought control.

Shepherding Your Thoughts   5 minutes

Choose a quite place with as few external distractions as possible, and sit facing a lit candle. Focus on the candlelight. As you sit, concentrating your attention on the flame, notice your thoughts. Simply notice them. And redirect your attention back to the flame. Notice yourself creating thoughts like, "how much longer am I going to do this?" or "I hope nobody's watching me, this is weird." Let those thoughts go, and bring your attention back to the flame. As you practice this, your thought awareness will rise noticeably. This exercise will strengthen your ability to catch your internal distractions sooner and manage them more effectively.

Paradoxical Intention

This tool is useful for those persistent "invaders", like those annoying songs that seem to infiltrate your brain and just won't go away. *Don't fight them!* That just gives them power. When you're dealing with one of those relentless internal distractions that's being entirely oppositional and defying your shepherding skills, try this.

Exaggerate the hell out of it. If you can't beat it by redirecting it, beat it by joining it—and join it like crazy. If it's a song, sing it out loud and absolutely destroy it. Exaggerate the words, the rhythm, and the volume (if you're somewhere where you can do that with minimal embarrassment!). Make a joke out of it. If the distraction is a thought of someone with whom you have some unfinished business, stop what you're doing momentarily and have a full-on dialog with that person. Give 'em hell. Let 'em have it! Exaggerate it enormously. Make it hilarious. Imagine a ridiculous scenario in which you get total resolution. Imagine it in detail. Do it twice. Smile. Then get back to work.

2. External Management

External distraction management is all about setting boundaries, for yourself and for others, and committing to keeping those boundaries firm. Managing externals involves committing to consistently executing all of your preventative measures (turning off phones, strategically scheduling times, beating distraction to the punch by satiating it in advance), and having enough conviction and dedication to your productivity to say "NO!" Prioritize your productivity. People who are especially vulnerable to distraction often under-prioritize their own desire to get things done and defer to the requests or demands of others' priorities. Practice setting boundaries with the people around you, and doing so repeatedly, until it gets easier and until you notice folks respecting your discipline and ceasing to distract you.

I have made it abundantly clear to my individual clients that Tuesdays are writing days, and I have done so consistently. All of them have very considerately acknowledged my boundary and have stopped requesting appointments on Tuesdays.

Elite athletes integrate mental prep routines into their pre-game preparation. This involves isolating from others and "going inside" for a while (putting on their game face, doing pre-game imagery, etc.) in order to create their perfect performance mindset going into the game. At first, these athletes must remind teammates that might approach them while they're executing their pre-game routines that they don't want to be interrupted for this 10 minute period of time and that they'll talk shortly. Soon, teammates learn to respect that ritual—give the player their space (stop distracting). Some even adopt the ritual for themselves.

Define your boundaries and honor them. Articulate them to the folks around you, and do it consistently.

3. <u>Picking Specific Targets and Rewarding Yourself</u>

When you are engaged in completing a certain task, set a specific goal to hit, determine the exact time to break or finish and decide on something with which to reward yourself for your effort when you're done. If the task is studying for an exam, for example, determine in advance that you will cover three chapters, you'll be finished by 9pm and afterwards you will reward yourself with an hour of your favorite TV show, recreational reading, or a phone call to a friend.

The key here is to remove ambiguity from your productivity goals by precisely clarifying in advance your benchmarks, your time commitment, and most definitely what's in it for you at the end.

Mental Stretching

"There is no expedient to which a man will not go to avoid the real labor of thinking."

—*Thomas Edison*

What is it?

Simply put, mental stretching is the psychological equivalent of physical stretching. It is the execution of mental conditioning drills that stretch the limits of your cognitive abilities. Stretching makes you tougher. Athletes stretch their muscles for several reasons:

- To increase range of motion
- To increase flexibility
- To decrease proneness to injury
- To increase power and speed

These are the same benefits you stand to gain—on a psychological level, of course—by incorporating mental stretching into your daily routine.

Why is it important?

Increased range of motion

Through stretching, your mind achieves a greater range of motion. That is, it can cover more territory. With an increased range of motion, more options and solutions become available to you. A greater range of motion equates to more possibilities. Creativity is enhanced. You experience a heightened quantity and quality of ideas.

Increased flexibility

The greater your flexibility, the greater your ability to adjust and respond to unpredictables. Conversely, the less flexible you are mentally (the more rigid), the less capable you are of dealing with surprises. Flexibility is the ability to respond skillfully to external forces or events.

Decreased proneness to "injury"

The more you stretch, the less likely you are to err. As you increase flexibility and range of motion, you become more efficient and more effective. Mistakes become more infrequent, and your range of error is narrowed.

Increased power and speed

Your action is more disciplined. Your presence has more impact. Your speech is more moving. Your influence is more profound. Your thinking is sharper and more rapid. Your memory is more acute. Your progress is more fluid. You're more relaxed and confident. You're significantly more productive.

How Do You Do It?

Create a habit of including some form of mental stretching into your daily routine. Mental stretching comes in many forms, so this need not be difficult. Examples of mental stretching exercises include:

word puzzles	visual art
brain teasers	creating music
riddles	mathematical equations
chess	meditation
cognitive exercises	

Any exercise that requires you to think—to actually think hard—qualifies as a mental stretch. There is no shortage of available mental stretching exercises. Every newspaper has crossword puzzles. Every bookstore has scads of books full of mental exercises. The Internet is full of mental stretching websites and exercises.

I want you to try the exercises on the following three pages. DO NOT worry about whether or not you complete them accurately, or if you complete them at all. The effort is what pays the dividends, not the outcome. That's very important! The stretching occurs in the effort you exert.

The value of mental stretching is in the exercising of thought—not the product of that thought.

Notice your thoughts as you contemplate whether or not you will even *try* some of these exercises.

"I just stink at these."
"Oh, man, that one will take forever. Forget it."
"I can't do that."

If you're thinking these things, or thoughts like them, you must have had some previous experience with exercises like these, and that experience was probably not fun. It is also safe to assume that previously you thought that puzzles and exercises like these were only valuable or enjoyable if you were able to solve them correctly. Forget your previous experience with exercises like these. Remember, the value is in the struggle. It's just like exercise. Your muscles grow when they're being pushed to their limits, not when they're relaxing. These exercises are designed to stretch your thinking to new limits. Solutions are secondary. *Effort* is of primary concern here. It is for that reason that the solutions to these puzzles do not appear in this book. If that becomes frustrating, change your thinking.

Exercise 1:

● ● ●

● ● ●

● ● ●

This is a very popular exercise. You very well may have seen this before. Regardless, do it. The limiting thought that prevents folks from seeing the solution the first time, very often returns to prevent them from seeing it the second and third times as well.

Using a pen or pencil, your task is to connect the 9 dots.
You may only use 4 lines, all of which must be straight.
You may not lift the pen or pencil from the page once you begin.
You may not back-trace.

This is not a trick. There is a simple solution (although that solution may not appear so simple at first).

Exercise 2:

You are walking on a path exiting the woods. On the horizon you see the skyline of a city. That city is your destination. Up ahead your path splits into two. You happen to know that one of these paths leads directly to the city, and that one does not. You don't know which is which. At the entrance to each path stands a man. You happen to know that one of them is a truth teller, and the other is a liar. You don't know which is which. You are permitted to ask one question, to one of the two men, and one question only. Your objective is to get to the city. What is the question that you ask?

Exercise 3:

You are standing in the first floor of a house. On the wall beside you is a light switch panel with three switches on it. Only one of the three is operative; the other two are disconnected. You don't know which is the operative switch, or which are inoperative. You do know that the one that works turns on a light in a closed, windowless closet upstairs. You cannot see the light from where you are standing. You must figure out which is the operative switch, but you are permitted only one trip upstairs. Assume that all switches are in the off position to start. How do you figure out which is the operative switch?

Exercise 4:

Think of an object that you've never thought of before!

This is not as simple as it sounds. Your task is to imagine some object—anything—that is completely original. By completely original, I mean something that is entirely unrelated to anything you have ever heard of, been aware of, sensed, encountered or experienced in any way to date. An orange half elephant half mouse, for example, is not an acceptable response as you have previously conceived of an elephant, a mouse, and the color orange. An engine that consumes air is not an acceptable response, as you are already conscious of the existence of both engines as well as air.

Exercise 5:

Your objective is to rearrange the pyramid so that it points downward. You may move only three dots.

Exercise 6:

Which number comes next in the series?

234 197 162 129 98

Exercise 7:

The grid has a numerical sequence in each column and row. Starting with the given numbers, fill in all the boxes. (Watch your thoughts right now!)

12				
		37		
			70	82
27				
		82		
47				

Trusting Timing

For the same reason that a farmer doesn't stand over his freshly planted seeds asking, "Where the hell are the plants?" nor should you fret over the often immediately undetectable results of your disciplined action. There is a certain perfect timing that dictates how and when things occur in this world—regardless of the amount and quality of your efforts. To maximize your efficiency, and more importantly, your sense of peace in this life, you must trust that timing. Anything to the contrary will result in counter-productivity and stress (which spirals into more counter-productivity).

Yes, miracles happen everyday. And, therefore, yes, it is definitely possible for rapid—or even immediate—spurts of enormous progress and achievement. And, therefore, we should strive for that sort of outcome while simultaneously accepting precisely what unfolds as perfectly timed.

This book is about creating your Dream in the most efficient way possible. Maximum efficiency can only be achieved through embracing timing.

"Hurry!"

"You should be further along than you are."

"Why haven't they called yet?!"

"I don't understand why this isn't working!"

"This shouldn't be happening!"

These are your thoughts. These are the statements made by your distrustful inner voice. This is the part of your brain that has been very effectively programmed to believe that when you don't get what you want exactly when you want it, then that's just bad. Well, it's that voice, and that programming that inspire you to make decisions that result in backfires. It's this sense of urgency that paradoxically ensures delayed gratification when you so desperately want it now.

This following example doesn't apply to you or I, *of course*, but we've all at least heard of situations like this! (If you've ever seen the movie *Swingers*, you'll recognize this as a slightly less exaggerated example of desperation ruining a potentially good thing.)

Your friend (we'll call him Johnny) meets a woman that he is very interested in romantically. For whatever combination of reasons, he is absolutely head over heels for this new love interest and he simply cannot wait to see if she's "the one." So he calls her the morning after he meets her and leaves her a voicemail. He doesn't hear back from her all day so he calls again in the early evening and gets her voice-mail again. He leaves another message. That's two. It's almost bed-time now and still no return call! Johnny contemplates making one more attempt before retiring for the night but something tells him maybe he shouldn't. (That something, by the way, is the most ingen-ious part of Johnny's brain, which he customarily ignores.) Instead he calls you. Because of your infinite wisdom, groundedness and complete understanding of the need to trust timing, you advise Johnny to chill out and give his new friend a chance to respond on her own time. He listens, thanks you sincerely for your brilliant guidance, hangs up, feels a certain sense of momentary serenity, lays down, starts to think about her, wonders why she hasn't called him back, ignores your brilliant guidance completely, gets up, makes the third call (at 11:30pm), gets her voicemail (she's home and knows damn well it's him again), leaves a pathetic message, and absolutely positively guarantees he'll never hear from her again.

Even though neither you nor I have ever been the Johnny in that scenario (of course!), it's a safe assumption that we've both had many similar sorts of situations in which we've created urgency around something important to us. We then permitted that urgency to guide our actions, and consequently destroyed any chances of getting what we wanted.

Urgency is the enemy. And it's an illusion!

Urgency is simply a sensation that is the product of undisciplined thinking.

There is no such thing as an urgent situation. Only urgent interpretations of situations exist.

> *"If you are distressed by anything external, the pain is not due to the thing itself but to your own estimate of it; and this you have the power to revoke at any moment."*
> —*Marcus Aurelius*

Immediately upon being planted, the farmer's seed begins to grow. We cannot see that, but our inability to detect the growth does not mean that growth is not happening. Take your disciplined action, and then trust—completely—that your action is producing results. You'll always have time later on to make adjustments to your action if you feel it's necessary.

No urgency.

Trust.

The Winner's Circle

"The glory of friendship is not in the outstretched hand, not the kindly smile nor the joy of companionship; it is the spiritual inspiration that comes to one when he discovers that someone else believes in him and is willing to trust him."
—*Ralph Waldo Emerson*

I could master every last Mental Toughness Tool in the book, I could achieve every last one of my professional and material goals, and I would have accomplished nothing if I did not also master the art of building relationships with amazing people that love me and support me.

The word "Winner" in The Winner's Circle refers to those people who succeed in surrounding themselves with a "circle" of friends that makes being who they are and doing what they do easier. Great friends are enzymes to the process of creating your Dream. More importantly, great friends make your life greater.

Emerson speaks to the inspiration that comes from being believed in and trusted. Although it is true that results provide reinforcement and motivation, and belief and enthusiasm are great sources of inspiration, the initiative and drive that come from a true friend's belief in you is unparalleled.

3 Steps to Creating Your Winner's Circle

1. Adopt an Abundant Mentality
2. Define Your High Standards
3. Take Inventory

1. Adopt an Abundant Mentality

There is a direct relationship between the kind of people you attract and the way you think. There is more than enough of everything in this life to go around, and that includes people to invite into your innermost circle—your tribe, so to speak. This is a mentality of abundance. People who think abundantly, live abundantly.

This is the first step in creating a Winner's Circle. Believe that there is an absolute abundance of great people—those who will love and support you—and that you are perfectly entitled to and deserved of having them in your circle. Obviously people have different preferences regarding how few or how many people they like to include in their circle. Regardless of the quantity, the first step is remembering that you can have precisely the quality of people you want to have in your life.

2. Define Your High Standards

The second step is to define your standards for the Winner's Circle. You must be clear on what you want in order to manifest it. Define the qualities you insist upon for your closest friends and settle for nothing less. Choose 5 ultimate attributes. Remember abundance: because great people are available to you, demand greatness.

Set your standards high. There is no healthy reason to include, or to continue to include, people that do not meet this standard in your Winner's Circle.

"It's a funny thing about life; if you refuse to accept anything but the best,
you very often get it."
—*W. Somerset Maugham*

3. Take Inventory

Step 3 is to take inventory of your current circle. Who are the people you consider to be your closest friends? Do they all meet your standard? If so, you've got yourself a solid Winner's Circle. If not, however, it's time to take some action. If none of the people listed meet each of your 5 standards, then it's time to attract some new folks. This does not necessarily mean that the friends you listed are not friends. They very well could be good friends. It does mean, however, that nobody on your list meets the standard for your Winner's Circle. And in that case, it's time for you to find some who do. How you accomplish this is far less important than keeping clear, as you do, that you are not simply looking for *more* friends. You are inviting **greatness** into your life. You are interested in attracting people who will honor you in precisely the way you want to be honored. This process could take months. Regardless of the length of time it takes to attract great people, continue to do it. Continue to think abundantly. Expect that you will succeed in creating your Winner's Circle.

Step 1: Adopt an Abundant Mentality

Remind yourself of this multiple times daily until it becomes a belief:

Great people are available to me.

Step 2: Define Your High Standards*

*As you determine your standards, imagine the *ideal* friend. Do not set your standards by selecting attributes of folks in your current circle. This may be challenging, as your current circle may be the easiest template for you to use. Do your best.

_____   _____   _____

_____   _____   _____

Step 3: Take Inventory of Your Current Circle

List the names of all the people you consider to be your closest friends. Go through the list to see how many, if any, of them possess each of the 5 ultimate attributes. This exercise may feel awkward to you. It may seem somewhat insensitive. It's not. This is an exercise in mindfulness and deservedness. Each of us deserves, completely, the privilege of the Winner's Circle. Many, many of us are settling for far less than that as a result of scarcity thinking—believing that there is *any* legitimate reason to not have a support network of the highest caliber.

Results of this exercise could include anything from reaffirming that you have a powerful Winner's Circle already, to clarifying that you not only have no true comrades, but also that you are in a situation where you actually have no friends at all. You may discover that there are folks that you have considered friends, who after closer consideration are actually not friends at all.

Regardless of the outcome of this exercise, remember that this is an exercise in making an objective assessment of the nature in which you have been including people in your life; it is an exercise in demanding greatness.

Negativity Immunity

This Mental Toughness Tool involves developing immunity to other people's negativity. So toward that end, let's define negativity as such:

negativity: any language—spoken, written, or body language—that asserts or implies you can't be who you want, do what you want, or have what you want.

As we humans evolve as a race, we are gradually becoming more mentally tough. At this particular stage in our development, however, extreme Mental Toughness is not the norm. Consequently, in our endeavors to create our Dreams, we customarily experience inordinate amounts of undisciplined thinking in the form of negativity from people with whom we interact or by which we are affected. Our own degree of Mental Toughness determines *how* we are affected by such negativity.

Even the most disciplined of minds at times are "guilty" of reinforcing limiting beliefs—albeit inadvertently. Conscious or unconscious, intentional or not, negative influences abound. For this reason, Negativity Immunity is an extremely valuable tool to have handy in your Mental Toughness toolbox.

There are 3 steps to strengthening your immunity to negativity:

1. **Acceptance: accepting the existence and prevalence of negativity without judgment or resistance.**

2. Recognition: rapidly recognizing negativity for what it is, and what it is not.

3. Utilization: utilizing—or at least neutralizing—negativity.

1. Acceptance

Resistance is futile! (I couldn't resist using that line here.) Negativity is not bad. It just is. And it *is* everywhere. But because it's not bad, that it's everywhere is OK. If you resist acknowledging and accepting its prevalence in your life, however, its influence upon you will be great. If, on the other hand, you embrace the existence of negativity, without judgment, you will strengthen your immunity to it.

2. Recognition

In order to utilize or neutralize negativity, you must first be able to recognize it rapidly, before it can influence your thinking and your actions. Negativity is nothing more than undisciplined thoughts and beliefs. Negativity is doubt. It is communicated in the form of negative language—spoken, written, or in body language.

It is important to recognize negativity as nothing more than language born of doubt.

Negativity is not a reflection of truth. Nor is it a reflection of a negative person. It is merely a reflection of negative beliefs learned by that person. By recognizing it as such, it becomes much easier to remain unaffected by it, or better yet, to manipulate it such that it works in your favor. Practice interpreting negative language this way from now on.

3. Utilization—or at least neutralization

By recognizing negative language as simply nothing more than a byproduct of a limiting belief that has gone unrecognized by the person who communicated it, you have already neutralized it. You are immune to its limiting effects. For example, suppose a member of your sales team discouragingly utters in a team meeting, "At this rate, we'll *never* make our quota." Although it may be accurate statement—if your team continues to perform at the current rate, it will fall short of the quota—it's a negative statement. The negativity arises out of the implication that the team will not accelerate its performance. You recognize this comment as nothing more than a product of a limiting belief. You remain unaffected by it. Your confidence in your own performance, as well as in the performance of the team, remains unaltered. That's good. That's neutralization.

In many cases like this, however, it is useful to go one step further than neutralization. You can actually *utilize* another's negative language by converting it into fuel. You can literally use that comment as a cue to exercise Mental Toughness. Use negativity as a reminder to create disciplined, empowering thoughts and beliefs of your own. Using the same example, "At this rate, we'll *never* make our quota," you can choose to interpret that in many ways. Here are a few:

"That's very true. So what we need to do is adjust the rate at which we're performing. Let's figure out how."

"That's actually not true. This is precisely the pace at which we were performing last quarter and we easily made quota."

"I have no idea if that's accurate or not, but I'm going to assume it's true and use it as motivation to set a personal performance record for this period."

These are possible interpretations that you could choose to think to yourself in response to another's negative language. You might even choose to articulate them to the team in this case. That, of course, would be up to you, but in either case, you have taken potentially contagious negativity and utilized it in a skillful and empowering way. That's discipline.

Examples of negativity recognized and utilized:

Situation: You are discussing your upcoming tennis match with one of your playing partners.

Negative: "You'll never beat her. She hasn't lost a match yet this season."

Recognize: Simply a limiting belief.

Utilize: "She hasn't played *me* yet this season!"

Situation: You are discussing with an acquaintance your plan to apply for a certain job or position.

Negative: "That would be a nice opportunity for you, but I don't think you're qualified. They're probably looking for someone with a lot more experience."

Recognize: Simply a limiting belief.

Utilize: Think: "I hope all my competition thinks like you!"

Situation: You present an idea to your supervisor.

Negative: "That's an interesting suggestion, but it's not very practical."

Recognize: Simply a limiting belief.

Utilize: Think: "Perfect! That's proof that I'm being creative and thinking big!"

THINK!

"Thinking is the hardest work there is,
which is the probable reason why so few people engage in it."
—*Henry Ford*

Make time to think. Create opportunities to do nothing other than sit and think. Put the stretching we spoke of earlier to use. Think about extraordinary people, places, and things. Think about what's great in your life. Think about the problems we face in our world today. Think about potential solutions to those problems. Think about yourself providing those solutions. Think big. You're never too busy to think. Make the time. Thinking is phenomenal mental exercise. Think about things you're not used to thinking about. Find a place, or several places, to do your thinking. Go to the beach, hike a mountain, go to a café, or use a quiet comfortable spot in your home. Put on some good thinking music. Maybe light some candles. Create a contemplative mood.

Think about things that make you curious. Think about things complex or foreign. Don't necessarily feel like you need to *do* anything with your thoughts or ideas. You can if you feel the inspiration to, but that's not the intention here. Just think. Consider this thinking practice. Get into the habit of giving your mind its own private time.

Our culture has grossly underemphasized the value and importance of developing our cognitive abilities. We're told things like, "you shouldn't think so much." What horrible advice. If you think you think too much, you're simply thinking in an undisciplined fashion. Change that. I translate "you think too much" into "you're thinking in a way that's disempowering" or "you're thinking the wrong things." Instead of abandoning your thinking entirely, simply change your method of thinking. Either change the content or change your perspective on the content. For example, there is nothing inherently unpleasant about contemplating a financially limiting situation. Suppose you are deep in debt. Being deep in debt is not bad. It may not be what you want for your life right now. It may not be how you want to continue to live, but it is not bad. It simply is. It is a fact. Information only. You want to change that fact. To think about your debt is not undisciplined. It is undisciplined if, and only if, you are choosing to think about your debt in a debilitating way. If you're only thinking things like, "This is horrible. I'll never get caught up. What an idiot I am. I'm so bad with money," then your thinking is extremely undisciplined. If you are avoiding thinking about it at all, this too is extremely undisciplined. If, on the other hand, you are choosing to contemplate your debt in a way that results in constructive ideas for action to get out of debt, then you're demonstrating Mental Toughness. "I have $X in student loan debt, $X in credit card debt, and $X in an auto loan to repay. That means my total debt is $X. In order to pay off all of my debt in 5 years, I will need to make $X in payments each month. In order to do that, I must increase my monthly income by $X. Now I'll create some action steps on accomplishing that." That is an emotionally empowering approach to thinking about something that most people feel paralyzed by as a result of undisciplined thinking strategies.

Remember, there is nothing you can think of that can, by itself, make you feel badly. You control how you interpret everything, which means you control how you feel—at all times. That means nothing is off limits for you to contemplate.

As you become more skilled at psychologically neutralizing adverse situations, the available content for your contemplative moments expands tremendously—infinitely, in fact.

Of course, you don't want to limit your thoughts to problems and their solutions. Make time to contemplate what's perfect in your life. Think about those things that are effortlessly exciting. Contemplate your successes. Contemplate the beauty of this moment. Curiously examine nature. Wonder and explore. Observe the world through the eyes of a child. Let your natural inquisitive nature take over for a while. Re-ignite your desire to ask, "why?"

Thinking is phenomenal exercise. Don't ever let anyone tell you, "You think too much."

The Secret Weapon: Your Mentor

What is a Mentor?

Your mentor is your secret weapon. Don't underestimate its power. A mentor is a person you include in your life for the specific intention of helping you grow more efficiently (doing things right) and more effectively (doing the right things). Your mentor must be someone for whom you have tremendous respect. Your mentor is your own personal advisor with whom you communicate regularly and who helps guide the process of creating your Dream.

The Value of a Mentor

Your mentor:

- accelerates your learning curve
- provides solid guidance and advice that is grounded in tremendous experience
- saves you time
- permits you to be in the student/learner/apprentice role (no matter how skilled they may be, the ultimate performers remain humble enough to continue to learn from the Masters that walked before them)

- provides a sense of added safety and security: when you feel stuck, you have them to turn to
- motivates you

Qualities of an Excellent Mentor

Your mentor:

- is an expert in your (or a very similar) field, and has achieved enormous success
- has phenomenal listening skills
- genuinely cares about you and your Dream
- takes a vested interest in your success
- avails themselves to you
- pushes you beyond your comfort zones—in order to help you to develop *personally* as well as professionally
- makes you think—forces you to exercise your mind
- promotes self-reliance and competence
- walks their talk
- genuinely *believes* in you

Finding your Mentor

- First, set you intention. Decide you will manifest an excellent mentor.
- Share your intention with the folks you know—you never know who knows who.

- Search and ask. Inquire with the people whose path you cross. Once you begin to put your intention out there, options will present themselves: "When the student is ready, the Master will come."

- Be selective. Don't settle. You'll know when you've got a good fit. Don't stop searching until you know.

Giving back

"When you cease to make a contribution, you begin to die."
—*Eleanor Roosevelt*

Giving back to the world is as much an act of discipline as it is an act of generosity. Not only is it altruistic, it's wise. Giving back to the world—or to your community—is a tactical move. It's the ultimate win-win, and for that reason, it is one of the most valuable Mental Toughness Tools in your toolbox.

As it is vital to the gymnast to maintain balance on beam, and as it is vital for the executive to maintain balance between work and family, so too is it vital for you to balance taking from this world what is rightfully yours with Giving back to this world what is rightfully yours.

Giving back keeps the flow going. The "flow" represents the flow of opportunity, affluence, friendship, love and everything else of value circulating among people. Giving back, and doing it well, requires the abundant mentality—the belief that there is more than enough of everything to go around. When you operate from the opposing mentality—the scarcity mentality—your actions are dictated by the fear that you will not have enough. This fear inspires hoarding, and hoarding clogs the flow. In their book, *The One Minute Millionaire*, Mark Victor Hansen and Robert Allen describe the characteristics and behavioral habits of "The Enlightened

Millionaire." One of these behaviors is tithing—contributing the first 10% of your earnings to charity. Why? To keep the flow going.

Today's networking gurus define networking as an opportunity to *give* folks what they need. This is entirely contrary to the popular notion that networking events are opportunities to *get* business. Paradoxically, when you think abundantly, you allow yourself to become genuinely interested in discovering what it is that people need or want, and then doing your best to help them get it. Such giving, consequently, inspires folks to give back to you. It's the perfect win-win.

Giving back can come in many forms. You can Give back your money, your time, your effort. Ask yourself, "How do I give back to the world right now?" If it requires effort to answer that, take action **right now** to change that. True Giving back involves some sacrifice. In order for it to be real giving, you've got to feel it a little. By that I mean it can't be effortless. It shouldn't create any suffering, of course, but it must involve a meaningful contribution. Dropping a can of vegetables into a collection box at the grocery store is a generous act, but it doesn't qualify as real Giving back. Making a mindful contribution of your time, effort, and/or money does. Ten percent of your earnings to a charity, one Saturday morning every month to a nonprofit organization, providing gratis service to people in need are forms of real Giving back.

Remember, the beauty of Giving back is the mutual benefit that results from it. You gain from giving. Giving back is not an obligation. It's an act of discipline that also happens to be an act of humanitarianism. Capitalize on that!

Great Expectations
and
Infinite Acceptance

It is impossible to expect too much! We use 10% of our brains, for Pete's sake! We can't even begin to fathom what we're capable of. So how, then, could we possibly ever set an expectation that was "too high"? We've all heard, "Oh, your expectations were too high," so may times after an unsuccessful attempt at something. What's the message in that statement? It's saying you didn't get what you wanted because you aren't capable enough. It's implying that the attempt has resulted in failure. And it often implies that you were foolish for ever even considering success as a possibility in the first place! That statement could only be a product of excessively undisciplined thinking. It's a classic example of a negative influence that you want to recognize right away and utilize. Here's a possible translation into disciplined thought:

> "You didn't get what you shot for. Way to go for trying, you Stud! Most people would never have the guts to even attempt that in your position. Let's figure out what worked, what didn't, and how you can nail it next time!"

The only reason people are reluctant to set high expectations is that they choose to interpret falling short as failure—as bad. There is no such thing as failure. There are only results. These folks haven't learned to accept unwanted outcomes as valuable information—and information only. Acceptance is what's missing. Acceptance is not to be confused with complacency.

Acceptance is a demonstration of power.

Complacency is a demonstration of powerlessness.

When you learn to accept all outcomes, entirely, as valuable sources of information and feedback, then you will be free. Free to set your expectations as high as any possibility you can conceive. And you will be free to go after those expectations with more conviction and commitment, more certainty and less hesitation than ever before. You will be free to perform without fear. Because you can't lose! That's freedom.

What you expect to achieve dictates your level of effort going into an event or performance. You can tell yourself a thousand times beforehand that you're going to give it your all, but unless you expect it all, you definitely won't be giving it your all.

There have been countless studies conducted to illustrate the power of expectation. In one of these studies, competitive weightlifters lifted upwards of 30% more weight than they had ever lifted before when fooled into believing the amount of weight they were attempting to lift was significantly less than it actually was.

The weightlifters performed according to the level of their expectations. In this particular study, deception was used to influence the weightlifters' levels of expectation. You, however, do not need deception. You simply need disciplined thought, and disciplined action.

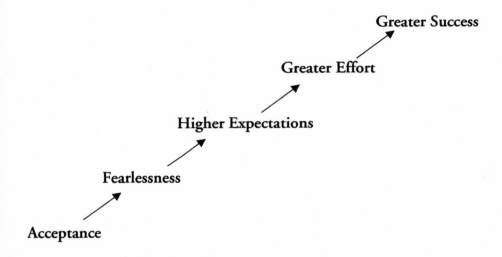

As you continue to practice disciplining your thinking, you strengthen your ability to accept outcomes as valuable information. As you accept more, you become more fearless. As you become more fearless, you elevate your expectations of yourself and your performance. As you elevate your expectations, your effort intensifies. As your effort level increases, so does your level of success.

Awareness & Presence

"He who knows much about others may be learned,
but he who understands himself is more intelligent.
He who controls others may be powerful,
but he who has mastered himself is mightier still."
—*Lao-Tzu, Tao te Ching*

Every moment is infinite bliss. It's not that each moment has the potential for infinite bliss—it *is* infinite bliss. This very moment is as perfect as any other moment you have encountered or ever will encounter. It doesn't necessarily feel like that, though, does it? Probably not. Why not? Because over time we've adopted thinking habits that make it easy to think otherwise. If you recall an absolutely wonderful memory right now, some spectacular moment or event from your past, chances are you're pretty clear that that moment was more blissful than this one. Yet neither of those two moments possesses anything the other doesn't. The only reason one seems more wonderful than the other is that you choose to interpret them that way. Remember Shakespeare's quote:

"There is nothing either good or bad, but thinking makes it so."

The memory may be one of achievement or success, or of a peaceful place or time, or of an interaction with a special person. Whatever the case may be, the event with that person, in that place, or that thing that happened wasn't any more spectacular than this moment is right now. Unless you're thinking it was.

The point here is not to take anything away from those amazing moments, but rather to give something to all the other "uneventful" moments of your life that make up the vast majority of your life— that pass without notice and without joy.

When you were an infant, you were infinitely aware and infinitely present. You couldn't help but be. You had not yet learned to be anything other than aware and present. For the purposes of creating your Dream, and experiencing joy every step of the way, it's high time to remember that.

Awareness and Presence go hand in hand. I am aware when I am present, and I am present when I am aware. In other words, when I am present in this moment (not lost in fantasy of the future or recollection of the past) then I can be conscious of what's happening now, of the beauty of this moment and of my thoughts. When I am not present (caught up in future fantasy or past recollection) I cannot be conscious or aware of what's happening now, of this moment's beauty, nor of my thoughts. When I am demonstrating awareness of what's happening now, of the beauty of this moment and of my thoughts, then I am also demonstrating presence. One does not exist without the other.

If every moment is equally blissful, then you might ask, "Why would you ever plan for the future or take any action to change your life from what it is now? If now is as perfect as when you achieve your Dream, or any element of it, then why even go to the effort of changing a damn thing?" Great question. The answer: because you want to, and because it's fun. That's the only reason why. It's certainly not because you *need* to. You don't need to. Isn't that great? We only do all we do because we want to. That's liberating!

It would be easy to mistake this book for a book entirely about doing. It certainly does present itself that way, doesn't it? In fact, in the beginning of it, in the How To Use This Book section, I strongly emphasize that it is not a book you simply read, but rather a book that you DO. Yes, it is a book about creating your Dream by *doing* things like: clarifying exactly what it is that you want, taking immediate action to create momentum, devising a Master Plan so that you have a deliberate approach, and developing Mental Toughness so that you strengthen that approach as you proceed. But why? Why all this stuff to do? Again, simply because you can and because it's fun. It's not that once you create your Dream, suddenly your life will be complete. It's not because only then will you find bliss. You've already got that.

Life isn't about doing; it's about being. All the exercises you've completed and all the tools you've read about and put into practice all serve a paradoxical function. They're exercises and tools in how to do things so that you can take back control of your mind, and consequently your life, so you can experience the bliss. So you can live without fear. So you can eliminate the unnecessary suffering. To be the person you want to be, to be the way you want to be. To be.

Be careful of the doing-addiction: getting so caught up in the process of doing—working, creating, planning, managing, coordinating, running around, maintaining, fixing—that you forget to be. If you're always doing and forgetting to be, then what's it all for? If you're only ever doing, even if all you do you do with absolute discipline and Mental Toughness, you'll certainly realize pieces of your Dream, but you'll never fully realize it because you'll be too busy doing to ever enjoy it. How ironic would that be? How familiar might that be already?

Here's a great story about the doing-addiction:

The American Tourist and Mexican Fisherman

Author Unknown

An American tourist was at the pier of a small coastal Mexican village when a small boat with just one fisherman docked.

Inside the small boat were several large yellowfin tuna. The tourist complimented the Mexican on the quality of his fish and asked how long it took to catch them.

The Mexican replied, "Only a little while."

The tourist then asked, "Why didn't you stay out longer and catch more fish?"

The Mexican said, "With this I have more than enough to support my family's needs."

The tourist then asked, "But what do you do with the rest of your time?"

The Mexican fisherman said, "I sleep late, fish a little, play with my children, take siesta with my wife, Maria, stroll into the village each evening where I sip wine and play guitar with my amigos, I have a full and busy life."

The tourist scoffed, "I can help you. You should spend more time fishing; and with the proceeds, buy a bigger boat. With the proceeds from the bigger boat you could buy several boats. Eventually you would have a fleet of fishing boats. Instead of selling your catch to a middleman you would sell directly to the processor; eventually opening your own cannery. You would control the product, processing and distribution. You could leave this small coastal fishing village and move to Mexico City, then Los Angeles and eventually New York where you could run your ever-expanding enterprise."

The Mexican fisherman asked, "But, how long will this all take?"

The tourist replied, "15 to 20 years."

"But what then?" asked the Mexican.

The tourist laughed and said, "That's the best part. When the time is right you would sell your company stock to the public and become very rich, you would make millions."

"Millions?…Then what?"

The American said, "Then you would retire. Move to a small coastal fishing village where you would sleep late, fish a little, play with your kids, take siesta with your wife, stroll to the village in the evenings where you could sip wine and play your guitar with your amigos."

The American is so addicted to doing, he was blind to the fact that the fisherman was already living his Dream. The fisherman was doing all the doing he wanted to do. His life was blissful. He was living his dream life. He had no desire or need to do more. To the American tourist—someone addicted to doing—this is incomprehensible. It just doesn't register. The notion of not doing more doesn't compute. Not only does the doing addict lose sight of the purpose of doing (where doing becomes the means to its own end—the vicious cycle), but it is also impossible for him to enjoy the bliss of every moment of the doing, because he has forgotten choice. He's doing because he believes he must. He is so unaware of his own beliefs and thoughts and behaviors that he can't even stop long enough to ask, "Is this what I want? Is all this doing satisfying me? Is this my choice?" That's not living. That's dying.

Only under one circumstance would the fisherman choose to do more—to stay out fishing longer, to catch more fish, to save for another boat. He would only do that if he *wanted* to. And if he so desired, then the doing would be blissful because it would be a product of his choice. Sure, he would have to do certain things he may prefer not to, like fuel the boat, pay for the fuel, buy bait, clean dried fish guts off the boat at the end of the day, for example. He may prefer that these things didn't have to get done, but they come with his choice—and that makes them OK, and he's OK with doing them. Everything involved is a product of his choice.

Awareness and Presence permit you to exercise choice. Awareness and Presence permit you to be *while* you're doing. Then, no matter where you are, or what you're doing, you can experience bliss.

No matter how far you've come in your life, no matter how much you've accomplished to this point, you're no better off than you were when you started. You may have more money, more things, more success stories, or a job that makes it easier to do what you want to do, but you've got no more opportunity to experience bliss now than you've ever had. For those of us who have had challenging pasts, and whose lives seem significantly more pleasant now, this may sound ridiculous. But it's not. Infinite joy has been there—accessible—the whole way. It's just easier to feel that joy under certain circumstances than others, that's for sure.

The point here, again, is not to take anything away from your greatness or the greatness of your accomplishments. They're all beautiful. The point—to the contrary—is to increase the amount of time in your life that you are able to experience what you typically only experience during those rare moments you call great. The whole point of mastering these Mental Toughness Tools, Awareness and Presence especially, is to make it even easier for you to feel that greatness more and more frequently, and to not need those rare moments of accomplishment and success in order to feel at peace and in bliss. The irony in all of this is that as you become more capable of not waiting for bliss, the more you'll experience those moments for which you previously waited!

Here are some excellent Awareness and Presence exercises to practice:

The Infinite Beauty of Now

What's great about this exercise is you can practice it anywhere, anytime. This exercise strengthens your awareness of the infinite beauty of every moment. It's a wonderful exercise to practice anytime, but particularly so when you're feeling down.

Every moment is full of beauty. As I'm writing this, I happen to be looking out the window watching seagulls fly into the sunset. I'm listening to Don Henley—music I absolutely love. I'm writing on things for which I am passionate. I'm wearing my favorite sweatshirt. I'm having no difficulty whatsoever experiencing the beauty of this moment. This one's easy. They're not all so simple. Last week I had the flu. No beauty there. Not for me. No sir. Saw none of it. I was just bitter. The beauty was there, of course. I just chose not to experience any of it. It takes more effort at certain times and under certain circumstances than others, but the beauty is always there.

Try it now. Recognize and experience some of the beauty of now. Look around for something beautiful. Listen for something. Smell it. Feel it. Taste it. Think it. It's there. Notice the beauty in the craftsmanship of a desk or a cabinet. Notice the beauty of someone's smile. Notice the beauty of a photo and the wonderful feelings that come with the thoughts and memories of the people or places in it. Notice the beauty of a bird singing, or of people laughing, of the wind. Notice the beauty of the smell of something cooking, a flower, perfume. Notice the beauty of the warmth of the sun, the texture of your clothes. Notice the beauty of the refreshing nature of a drink of water. Notice the beauty of the old man walking slowly, children playing, the cat sleeping, the tree swaying, reflections and prisms of light. Notice the beauty of the excitement and peacefulness you feel right now as you acknowledge your power and your greatness.

The beauty is always there, like a guardian angel. It never goes away. Practice noticing more of it, more often. Raise your awareness to the infinite beauty of now.

Breathing

There is no simpler exercise in being present than breathing. By taking just a few moments to become aware of your breath and to breathe deeply and deliberately, you remove muscle tension and slow brain activity. The result: relaxation and presence.

This is another very versatile exercise. You can practice it anywhere. Take a controlled, slowly paced deep breath—down into your abdomen and slowly exhale. Repeat that a few times, and as you do, concentrate on inhaling beauty or peacefulness, confidence, serenity or anything else pleasant, and exhaling tension, fear, anger, or anything else unpleasant.

Slowing Down

Our culture moves so fast, it's easy to catch ourselves up in rushing even when we don't need to (we never actually *need* to). In fact, many of us spend most of our waking hours rushing—feeling pressured by time, hurrying, often for no apparent reason. Break this stressful, mindless habit by literally practicing slowing down throughout the course of the day. Deliberately walk slowly. Drive slower. Write slower. Speak slower. There's no hurry. Slow down.

Read the paragraph below, and then determine the number of times the letter "f" appears in it.

> FINISHED FILES ARE THE RE-
> SULT OF YEARS OF SCIENTIF-
> IC STUDY COMBINED WITH THE
> EXPERIENCE OF MANY YEARS.

How many did you come up with? The answer is six. There are six f's. Make sure you notice the three times the word "of" appears.

Those are easy to skip. Especially if you're rushing. What else do we miss every day as a result of rushing through it?

Shepherding Your Thoughts

This is an exercise in both thought awareness and staying present. Light a candle and set it in front of you. Concentrate all of your attention upon the candlelight. The task is to notice your wandering thoughts and to bring them back and refocus on the candlelight.

Think of your thoughts as a flock of sheep whose nature is to wander. You are the shepherd. Your job is to make sure the sheep don't wander off. When one does, you must notice it, stop what you're doing, and bring it back.

As you focus upon the candlelight, notice how you begin to think things like: "how long am I going to do this?" Notice the thought and refocus on the light. "Did I ever put the wash in the dryer?" Notice it. Bring it back. "I wish that dog would shut up." Notice it. "How's this supposed to help me?" Notice it. Bring it back. Do this for 5 minutes.

The Mindfulness Meal

Here's a wonderful Awareness and Presence exercise that you can practice while enjoying food!

Give yourself at least an hour for this one. I like to eat out for this exercise, but you certainly don't need to. It involves eating an entire meal as deliberately and on purpose as possible. What that means is you'll be noticing this meal in a way that you're likely not very accustomed to doing.

Once your meal is prepared, and you've sat down, proceed to eat, but don't swallow one single bite or sip without first experiencing it completely with each of your senses. Notice, in extreme detail, what the bite looks like. Notice its colors and its shapes. Notice the sound of the drink in the glass or the knife cutting. Notice the aromas. All of them. Notice the texture of the food on your tongue—without biting it yet. Notice the sensation of the desire to chew. Notice its taste and the details of its flavor as you chew it. And finally notice the sensation of swallowing it.

That's a whole new world of eating! Especially for those of us who are used to shoveling it down.

Reading

There is an abundance of great literature out there on Awareness and Presence. Here is a list of some of my favorites:

The Tao Te Ching	Lao-Tzu
The Power of Now	Eckhart Tolle
Zen and the Art of Motorcycle Maintenance	Robert Pirsig
The Art of Happiness	Dalai Lama and Howard C. Cutler
The Tao of Pooh	Benjamin Hoff
The Te of Piglet	Benjamin Hoff
After the Ecstasy, the Laundry: How the Heart Grows Wise on the Spiritual Path	Jack Kornfield

Revising the Map

Everything and everyone is constantly evolving. We change. Our priorities change, our bodies change, our situations change, our environments change. Our Dreams change, and thus, so must our Master Plans—or our "roadmaps" to those Dreams. We must take some time every so often to revise our maps and keep them current. As we accomplish our goals and as we change, our maps become obsolete and consciously or unconsciously we tend to abandon them. In fact, sometimes long before our Master Plans become obsolete, for various reasons we sidetrack ourselves or lose momentum. Of course, as we practice the Mental Toughness Tools, this happens less and less. But given that we're human, and that we're not yet infinitely aware and present, we're going to lose focus at times on certain things. We'll even lose our focus on things that are very important to us. Our lives are so stimulus saturated, we have so much going on, it's virtually impossible to maintain perfect focus upon, and perfect momentum for everything on our Dream lists. It's normal, so let's work with it.

What do you do when you notice that you've gone off course and lost your momentum on some, or even all of your Dream? Your first step is to remember to interpret that in a disciplined way. Remember, it ain't bad—just is. But it's not what you want so you'll change it. The second step, start over. Simply repeat the whole process. Go back to Step 1: Recreate The Dream. It may be very similar to the initial one. It might be entirely new. It'll probably be somewhere in between. In any case, it'll be fresh. Then follow the steps: Take immediate action on a few of your new Dream list items, and finally create Master Plans for your newly revised priorities.

Do this every six months or so. In six months you may have accomplished several of your short term intentions. Or maybe you'll be well underway with some of them, and it may be time to replace them on the list with new ideas, or it may not. Maybe it'll be time to simply be. That's the infinite beauty of that moment: you can choose. As you proceed in realizing your Dream you'll always have the option of choosing new and exciting things to add to your lists, or to simply enjoy your life exactly and precisely as it is.

Naturally, the longer term items on your Dream list will take longer to realize. Use this six month revision as a way to monitor your momentum on those items, or, more importantly, to reassess their importance in your life. It's entirely possible that as a consequence of circumstances and events that were impossible to predict six months prior, something that was formerly a priority no longer is. The only things that belong on your Dream list and in your Master Plans are things you *want* there—not things that have been there for a while. It doesn't matter if you've had becoming a concert pianist on your Dream list for three years. If it no longer gets your juices flowing, your heart's not in it. Let it go. To keep something around because it's been around is undisciplined. It's clutter. Exercise your Mental Toughness and your choice. Choose to keep only that which you genuinely care about.

You may want to literally schedule time six months from now to revise your map. Put it in your calendar. Enlist the help of a loved one, a friend, or your mentor to remind you and hold you account-able to this. Do what it takes to keep your momentum flowing for as long as you want it to flow.

Conclusion

*"The beginning of a habit is like an invisible thread, but
every time we repeat the act we strengthen the strand, add to
it another filament, until it becomes a great cable and binds
us irrevocably, thought and act."*

—*Orison Swett Marden*

Perseverance and trust. Prioritize them. Once you've clarified what your Dream is and created some forward progress, perseverance and trust will be your greatest assets. As long as you still want something, don't give up on it. Ever. Better to go to your grave having thoroughly enjoyed the process of striving for something wonderful and never having achieved it, than to settle for accomplishing things unimportant. When you are *being* as you are *doing*, you can't lose. If you remember that, it will be much easier to persevere through tougher times when it appears that things aren't working out.

And trust. Trust as the farmer trusts that his seeds will grow. When you can't detect progress, trust your method. Progress is not always visible. But as long as you are clear on your Dream and your plan, progress is happening. You can count on that. As long as you still want it, don't give up on it. Ever.

There is nothing more rewarding for me in this world than assisting someone in accomplishing their Dream. To help someone shed fear and situate enthusiasm and joy firmly in its place is my ultimate bliss.

It was my intention in writing this book to help you do just that. I sincerely hope you found this helpful.

Here's to your Dream!